The Complete
Psychotherapy Treatment
Planner

The Complete
Psychotherapy Treatment
Planner

Arthur E. Jongsma, Jr.

L. Mark Peterson

A Wiley-Interscience Publication
JOHN WILEY & SONS, INC.
New York • Chichester • Brisbane • Toronto • Singapore

Library of Congress Cataloging-in-Publication Data:

Jongsma, Arthur E., 1943–
    The complete psychotherapy treatment planner / by Arthur
  E. Jongsma, Jr., L. Mark Peterson.
        p.   cm.
    Includes bibliographical references.
    ISBN 0-471-11738-2 (pbk.)
    1. Mental illness—Treatment—Planning.   2. Psychiatric records.
  I. Peterson, L. Mark.   II. Title.
  RC480.5.J664   1995
  616.89'14'068—dc20   94-37096

Printed in the United States of America

15 14

CONTENTS

The Complete
Psychotherapy Treatment
Planner

INTRODUCTION

Since the early 1960s, formalized treatment planning has gradually become a vital aspect of the entire health-care delivery system, whether it is treatment related to physical health, mental health, child welfare, or substance abuse. What started in the medical sector in the 1960s spread into the mental health sector in the 1970s as clinics, psychiatric hospitals, agencies, and so on, began to seek accreditation from bodies such as the Joint Commission on Accreditation of Healthcare Organizations (JCAHO) to qualify for third-party reimbursements. For most treatment providers to achieve accreditation, they had to begin developing and strengthening their documentation skills in the area of treatment planning. Previously, most mental health and substance abuse treatment providers had, at best, a "bare-bones" plan that looked similar for most of the individuals they treated. As a result, clients were uncertain as to what they were trying to attain in mental health treatment. Goals were vague, objectives were nonexistent, and interventions were applied equally to all clients. Outcome data were not measurable, and neither the treatment provider nor the client knew exactly when treatment was complete. The initial development of rudimentary treatment plans made inroads toward addressing some of these issues.

With the advent of managed care in the 1980s, treatment planning has taken on even more importance. Managed care systems *insist* that clinicians move rapidly from assessment of the problem to the formulation and implementation of the treatment plan. The goal of most managed care companies is to expedite the treatment process by prompting the client and treatment provider to focus on identifying and changing behavioral problems as quickly as possible. Treatment plans must be specific as to the problems and interventions, individualized to meet the client's needs and goals, and measurable in terms of setting milestones that can be used to chart the patient's progress. Pressure from third-party payers, accrediting agencies, and other outside parties has therefore increased the need for clinicians to produce effective, high-quality treatment plans in a short time frame. However, many mental health providers have little experience in treatment plan development. Our purpose in writing this book is to clarify, simplify, and accelerate the treatment planning process.

TREATMENT PLAN UTILITY

Detailed written treatment plans can benefit not only the client, therapist, treatment team, insurance community, and treatment agency, but also the overall psychotherapy profession. The client is served by a written plan because it stipulates the issues that are the focus of the treatment process. It is very easy for both provider and client to lose sight of what the issues were that brought the patient into therapy. The treatment plan is a guide that structures the focus of the therapeutic contract. Since issues can change as therapy progresses, the treatment plan must be viewed as a dynamic document that can and must be updated to reflect any major change of problem, definition, goal, objective, or intervention.

Clients and therapists benefit from the treatment plan, which forces both to think about therapy outcomes. Behaviorally stated, measurable objectives clearly focus the treatment endeavor. Clients no longer have to wonder what therapy is trying to accomplish. Clear objectives also allow the patient to channel effort into specific changes that will lead to the long-term goal of problem resolution. Therapy is no longer a vague contract to just talk honestly and openly about emotions and cognitions until the client feels better. Both client and therapist are concentrating on specifically stated objectives using specific interventions.

Providers are aided by treatment plans because they are forced to think analytically and critically about therapeutic interventions that are best suited for objective attainment for the patient. Therapists were traditionally trained to "follow the patient," but now a formalized plan is the guide to the treatment process. The therapist must give advance attention to the technique, approach, assignment, or cathartic target that will form the basis for interventions.

Clinicians benefit from clear documentation of treatment because it provides a measure of added protection from possible patient litigation. Malpractice suits are increasing in frequency and insurance premiums are soaring. The first line of defense against allegations is a complete clinical record detailing the treatment process. A written, individualized, formal treatment plan that is the guideline for the therapeutic process, that has been reviewed and signed by the client, and that is coupled with problem-oriented progress notes is a powerful defense against exaggerated or false claims.

A well-crafted treatment plan that clearly stipulates presenting problems and intervention strategies facilitates the treatment process carried out by team members in inpatient, residential, or intensive outpatient settings. Good communication between team members about what approach is being implemented and who is responsible for which intervention is critical. Team meetings to discuss patient treatment used to be the only source of interaction between providers; often, therapeutic conclusions or assignments were not recorded. Now, a thorough treatment plan stipulates in writing the details of objectives and the varied interventions (pharmacologic, milieu, group therapy, didactic, recreational, individual therapy, etc.) and who will implement them.

Every treatment agency or institution is constantly looking for ways to increase the quality and uniformity of the documentation in the clinical record. A standardized, written treatment plan with problem definitions, goals, objectives, and interventions in every client's file enhances that uniformity of documentation. This uniformity eases the task of record reviewers inside and outside the agency. Outside reviewers, such as JCAHO, insist on documentation that clearly outlines assessment, treatment, progress, and discharge status.

The demand for accountability from third-party payers and health maintenance organizations (HMOs) is partially satisfied by a written treatment plan and complete progress notes. More and more managed care systems are demanding a structured therapeutic contract that has measurable objectives and explicit interventions. Clinicians cannot avoid this move toward being accountable to those outside the treatment process.

The psychotherapy profession stands to benefit from the use of more precise, measurable objectives to evaluate success in mental health treatment. With the advent of detailed treatment plans, outcome data can be more easily collected for interventions that are effective in achieving specific goals.

HOW TO DEVELOP A TREATMENT PLAN

The process of developing a treatment plan involves a logical series of steps that build on each other much like constructing a house. The foundation of any effective treatment plan is the data gathered in a thorough biopsychosocial assessment. As the client presents himself or herself for treatment, the clinician must sensitively listen to and understand what the client struggles with in terms of family of origin issues, current stressors, emotional status, social network, physical health, coping skills, interpersonal conflicts, self-esteem, and so on. Assessment data may be gathered from a social history, physical exam, clinical interview, psychological testing, or contact with a client's significant others. The integration of the data by the clinician or the multidisciplinary treatment team members is critical for understanding the client, as is an awareness of the basis of the client's struggle. We have identified six specific steps for developing an effective treatment plan based on the assessment data.

Step One: Problem Selection

Although the client may discuss a variety of issues during the assessment, the clinician must ferret out the most significant problems on which to focus the treatment process. Usually a *primary* problem will surface, and *secondary* problems may also be evident. Some *other* problems may have to be set aside as not urgent enough to require treatment at this time. An effective treatment plan can only deal with a few selected problems or treatment will lose its direction. This *Planner* offers thirty-four problems from which to select those that most accurately represent your client's presenting issues.

As the problems to be selected become clear to the clinician or the treatment team, it is important to include opinions from the client as to his or her prioritization of issues for which help is being sought. A client's motivation to participate in and cooperate with the treatment process depends, to some extent, on the degree to which treatment addresses his or her greatest needs.

Step Two: Problem Definition

Each individual client presents with unique nuances as to how a problem behaviorally reveals itself in his or her life. Therefore, each problem that is selected for treatment focus requires a specific definition about how it is evidenced in the particular client. The symptom pattern should be associated with diagnostic criteria and codes such as those found in the *Diagnostic and Statistical Manual* or the *International Classification of Diseases*. The *Planner*, following the pattern established by DSM-IV, offers such behaviorally specific definition statements to choose from or to serve as a model for your own personally crafted statements. You will find several behavior symptoms or syndromes listed that may characterize one of the thirty-four presenting problems.

Step Three: Goal Development

The next step in treatment plan development is that of setting broad goals for the resolution of the target problem. These statements need not be crafted in measurable terms but can be global, long-term goals that indicate a desired positive outcome to the treatment procedures. The *Planner* suggests several possible goal statements for each problem, but one statement is all that is required in a treatment plan.

Step Four: Objective Construction

In contrast to long-term goals, objectives must be stated in behaviorally measurable language. It must be clear when the client has achieved the established objectives; therefore, vague, subjective objectives are not acceptable. Review agencies (e.g., JCAHO), HMOs, and managed care organizations insist that psychological treatment outcome be measurable. The objectives presented in this *Planner* are designed to meet this demand for accountability. Numerous alternatives are presented to allow construction of a variety of treatment plan possibilities for the same presenting problem. The clinician must exercise professional judgment as to which objectives are most appropriate for a given client.

Each objective should be developed as a step toward attaining the broad treatment goal. In essence, objectives can be thought of as a series of steps that, when completed, will result in the achievement of the long-term goal. There should be at least two objectives for each problem, but the clinician may construct as many as are necessary for goal achievement. Target attainment dates should be listed for each objective. New objectives should be added to the plan as the individual's treatment progresses. When all the necessary objectives have been achieved, the client should have resolved the target problem successfully.

Step Five: Intervention Creation

Interventions are the actions of the clinician designed to help the client complete the objectives. There should be at least one intervention for every objective. If the client does not accomplish the objective after the initial intervention, new interventions should be added to the plan.

Interventions should be selected on the basis of the client's needs and the treatment provider's full therapeutic repertoire. This *Planner* contains interventions from a broad range of therapeutic approaches, including cognitive, dynamic, behavioral, pharmacologic, family-oriented, and solution-focused brief therapy. Other interventions may be written by the provider to reflect his or her own training and experience. The addition of new problems, definitions, goals, objectives, and interventions to those found in the *Planner* is encouraged because doing so adds to the database for future reference and use.

Some suggested interventions listed in the *Planner* refer to specific books that can be assigned to the client for adjunctive bibliotherapy. Appendix A contains a full bibliographic reference list of these materials. The books are arranged under each problem for which they are appropriate as assigned reading for clients. When a book is used as part of an intervention plan, it should be reviewed with the client after it is read, enhancing the application of the content of the book to the specific client's circumstances. For further information about self-help books, mental health professionals may wish to consult *The Authoritative Guide to Self-Help Books* (1994) by Santrock, Minnett, and Campbell (available from The Guilford Press, New York, NY).

Assigning an intervention to a specific provider is most relevant if the patient is being treated by a team in an inpatient, residential, or intensive outpatient setting. Within these settings, personnel other than the primary clinician may be responsible for implementing a specific intervention. Review agencies require that the responsible provider's name be stipulated for every intervention.

Step Six: Diagnosis Determination

The determination of an appropriate diagnosis is based on an evaluation of the client's complete clinical presentation. The clinician must compare the behavioral, cognitive, emotional, and interpersonal symptoms that the client presents to the criteria for diagnosis of a mental illness condition as described in DSM-IV. The issue of differential diagnosis is admittedly a difficult one that research has shown to have rather low inter-rater reliability. Psychologists have also been trained to think more in terms of maladaptive behavior than disease labels. In spite of these factors, diagnosis is a reality that exists in the world of mental health care and it is a necessity for third party reimbursement. (However, recently, managed care agencies are more interested in behavioral indices that are exhibited by the client than the actual diagnosis.) It is the clinician's thorough knowledge of DSM-IV criteria and a complete understanding of the client assessment data that contribute to the most reliable, valid diagnosis. An accurate assessment of behavioral indicators will also contribute to more effective treatment planning.

HOW TO USE THIS PLANNER

Our experience has taught us that learning the skills of effective treatment plan writing can be a tedious and difficult process for many clinicians. It is more stressful to try to develop this expertise when under the pressure of increased patient load and short time frames placed on clinicians today by managed care systems. The documentation demands can be overwhelming when we must move quickly from assessment to treatment plan to progress notes. In the process, we must be very specific about how and when objectives can be achieved, and how progress is exhibited in each client. *The Complete Psychotherapy Treatment Planner* was developed as a tool to aid clinicians in writing a treatment plan in a rapid manner that is clear, specific, and highly individualized according to the following progression:

1. Choose one presenting problem (Step One) you have identified through your assessment process. Locate the corresponding page number for that problem in the *Planner*'s table of contents.
2. Select two or three of the listed behavioral definitions (Step Two) and record them in the appropriate section on your treatment plan form. Feel free to add your own defining statement if you determine that your client's behavioral manifestation of the identified problem is not listed. (Note that while our design for treatment planning is vertical, it will work equally well on plan forms formatted horizontally.)
3. Select a single long-term goal (Step Three) and again write the selection, exactly as it is written in the *Planner* or in some appropriately modified form, in the corresponding area of your own form.
4. Review the listed objectives for this problem and select the ones that you judge to be clinically indicated for your client (Step Four). Remember, it is recommended that you select at least two objectives for each problem. Add a target date or the number of sessions allocated for the attainment of each objective.
5. Choose relevant interventions (Step Five). The *Planner* offers suggested interventions related to each objective in the parentheses following the objective statement. But do not limit yourself to those interventions. The entire list is eclectic and may offer options that are more tailored to your theoretical approach or preferred way of working with clients. Also, just as with definitions, goals, and objectives, there is space allowed for you to enter your own interventions into the *Planner.* This allows you to refer to these entries when you create a plan around this prob-

lem in the future. You will have to assign responsibility to a specific person for implementation of each intervention if the treatment is being carried out by a multidisciplinary team.

6. Several DSM-IV diagnoses are listed at the end of each chapter that are commonly associated with a client who has this problem. These diagnoses are meant to be suggestions for clinical consideration. Select a diagnosis listed or assign a more appropriate choice from the DSM-IV (Step Six).

   Note: To accommodate those practitioners that tend to plan treatment in terms of diagnostic labels rather than presenting problems, Appendix B lists all of the DSM-IV diagnoses that have been presented in the various presenting problem chapters as suggestions for consideration. Each diagnosis is followed by the presenting problem that has been associated with that diagnosis. The provider may look up the presenting problems for a selected diagnosis to review definitions, goals, objectives, and interventions that may be appropriate for their clients with that diagnosis.

Congratulations! You should now have a complete, individualized treatment plan that is ready for immediate implementation and presentation to the client. It should resemble the format of the sample plan presented on the facing page.

A FINAL NOTE

One important aspect of effective treatment planning is that each plan should be tailored to the individual client's problems and needs. Treatment plans should not be mass produced, even if clients have similar problems. The individual's strengths and weaknesses, unique stressors, social network, family circumstances, and symptom patterns *must* be considered in developing a treatment strategy. Drawing upon our own years of clinical experience, we have put together a variety of treatment choices. These statements can be combined in thousands of permutations to develop detailed treatment plans. Relying on their own good judgment, clinicians can easily select the statements that are appropriate for the individuals they are treating. In addition, we encourage readers to add their own definitions, goals, objectives, and interventions to the existing samples. It is our hope that *The Complete Psychotherapy Treatment Planner* will promote effective, creative treatment planning—a process that will ultimately benefit the client, clinician, and mental health community.

SAMPLE TREATMENT PLAN

Problem: ANGER MANAGEMENT

Definition: An overreaction of hostility to insignificant irritants. Use of verbally abusive language when talking to or about others.
History of explosive aggressive outbursts out of proportion to any precipitating stressors leading to assaultive acts or destruction of property.

Goals: Develop an awareness of current angry behaviors, clarifying origins of and alternatives to aggressive anger.

Objectives	Interventions
1. Increase awareness of anger expression patterns (4/20/95).	1. Confront/reflect angry behaviors in group and individual sessions.
	2. Assign client to read the book *Of Course You're Angry* (Rosellini and Worden).
2. Identify pain and hurt of past or current life that fuels anger (5/29/95).	1. Assign client to list experiences of life that have hurt and led to anger.
3. Develop specific, socially acceptable, non-self-defeating ways to handle angry feelings (6/20/95).	1. Assign assertiveness training classes.
	2. Work with client in individual therapy sessions, using role-playing techniques, to develop non-self-defeating ways of handling angry feelings.

Diagnosis: 312.34   Intermittent Explosive Disorder

ANGER MANAGEMENT

BEHAVIORAL DEFINITIONS

1. History of explosive aggressive outbursts out of proportion to any precipitating stressors leading to assaultive acts or destruction of property.
2. Overreaction of hostility to insignificant irritants.
3. Swift and harsh judgment statements made to or about others.
4. Body language of tense muscles (e.g., clenched fist or jaw, glaring looks, or refusal to make eye contact).
5. Use of passive-aggressive patterns (social withdrawal due to anger, lack of complete or timely compliance in following directions or rules, complaining about authority figures behind their backs, or nonparticipation in meeting expected behavioral norms).
6. Consistent pattern of challenging or disrespectful treatment of authority figures.
7. Use of verbally abusive language.

LONG-TERM GOALS

1. Decrease overall intensity and frequency of angry feelings and increase ability to recognize and appropriately express angry feelings as they occur.

2. Develop awareness of current angry behaviors, clarifying origins of and alternatives to aggressive anger.
3. Come to an awareness and acceptance of angry feelings while developing better control and more serenity.

—. _____

_____

—. _____

_____

—. _____

_____

SHORT-TERM OBJECTIVES

1. Increase awareness of anger expression patterns. (1, 12)
2. Identify pain and hurt of past or current life that fuels anger. (2, 3, 10)
3. Verbalize feelings of anger in a controlled, assertive way. (4, 11)
4. Verbalize an understanding of the need for a process of forgiveness of others and self to reduce anger. (5, 6, 9)
5. Decrease the number and duration of angry outbursts. (1, 10, 11, 12)
6. Identify targets of and causes for anger. (2, 7, 8, 10)
7. Increase awareness of how past ways of handling angry feelings have had a negative impact. (2, 3, 7, 10)

THERAPEUTIC INTERVENTIONS

1. Confront/reflect angry behaviors in group and individual sessions.
2. Assign client to list experiences of life that have hurt and led to anger.
3. Empathize and clarify feelings of hurt and anger tied to traumas of past.
4. Assign assertiveness training classes.
5. Discuss forgiveness of perpetrators of pain as a process of "letting go" of anger.
6. Assign client to read the book *Forgive and Forget* (Smedes).
7. Assign client to read the book *Of Course You're Angry* (Rosellini and Worden) or *The Angry Book* (Rubin).

The numbers in parentheses accompanying the short-term objectives correspond to the list of suggested therapeutic interventions.

8. Develop specific, socially acceptable and non-self-defeating ways to handle angry feelings. (4, 11)

9. Decrease verbal and physical manifestations of anger, aggression, or violence while increasing awareness and acceptance of feelings. (1, 4, 10, 12)

—. _____

_____

_____

—. _____

_____

_____

—. _____

_____

_____

8. Ask client to write an angry letter to parents, spouse, or whomever, focusing on the reasons for his/her anger toward that person.

9. Ask client to write a forgiving letter to target of anger as step toward letting go of anger.

10. Assign and process a thorough list of all targets and causes for anger.

11. Work with client in individual therapy sessions, using role-playing techniques, to develop non-self-defeating ways of handling angry feelings.

12. Process client's angry feelings or angry outbursts that have recently occurred and review alternative behaviors available.

—. _____

_____

_____

—. _____

_____

_____

—. _____

_____

_____

DIAGNOSTIC SUGGESTIONS

Axis I: 312.34   Intermittent Explosive Disorder
296.xx   Bipolar I Disorder
296.89   Bipolar II Disorder
312.81   Conduct Disorder/Childhood-Onset Type
312.82   Conduct Disorder/Adolescent-Onset Type
310.1   Personality Change Due to (Axis III Disorder)
309.81   Posttraumatic Stress Disorder

_____   _____

_____   _____

Axis II: 301.83   Borderline Personality Disorder
301.7   Antisocial Personality Disorder
301.0   Paranoid Personality Disorder
301.81   Narcissistic Personality Disorder
301.9   Personality Disorder NOS

_____   _____

_____   _____

ANTISOCIAL BEHAVIOR

BEHAVIORAL DEFINITIONS

1. An adolescent history of consistent rule-breaking, lying, physical aggression, disrespect for others and their property, stealing and/or substance abuse resulting in frequent confrontation with authority.
2. Consistent pattern of blaming others for what happens to him/her.
3. Refusal to follow rules with the attitude that they apply to others, not him/her.
4. History of reckless behaviors that reflect a lack of regard for self or others and show a high need for excitement, having fun, and living on the edge.
5. Little regard for truth as reflected in a pattern of consistently lying to and/or conning others.
6. A sexually promiscuous pattern; has never been totally monogamous in any relationship for a year and does not take responsibility for children.
7. A pattern of interacting in an irritable, aggressive, and/or argumentative way with authority figures.
8. Little or no remorse for hurtful behavior.
9. Verbal or physical fighting often initiated.
10. Failure to conform with social norms with respect to the law as shown by repeatedly performed antisocial acts that they may or may not have been arrested for (e.g., destroying property, stealing, pursuing an illegal job).
11. Pattern of impulsive behaviors, such as moving often, traveling with no goal, quitting a job without having another.
12. Inability to sustain behavior that would maintain consistent employment.
13. Failure to function as a consistently concerned and responsible parent.

—. _____

_____

—.   _____

      _____

—.   _____

      _____

LONG-TERM GOALS

1. Become more responsible for behavior and keep behavior within the acceptable limits of the rules of society.
2. Begin to develop and demonstrate a healthy sense of respect for social norms, the rights of others, and the need for honesty.
3. Improve method of relating to the world, especially authority figures; be more realistic, less defiant, and more socially sensitive.
4. Come to an understanding and acceptance of the need for limits and boundaries on behavior.

—.   _____

      _____

—.   _____

      _____

—.   _____

      _____

SHORT-TERM OBJECTIVES

1. Verbally demonstrate an understanding of the rules related to job, program, and so on. (1)
2. Consistently follow all rules. (1, 6, 8)
3. Identify the consequences that failure to comply with rules/limits has had on self and others. (2, 9, 10)
4. Receive feedback/redirection from staff/therapist with minimal resistance or argument. (2, 3, 6, 8)
5. Increase statements of accepting responsibility for behavior. (3, 5, 7, 8)
6. Decrease statements of blame of others or circumstances for own behavior, thoughts, and feelings. (5, 7, 8)
7. Verbalize increased level of awareness of rebellious behavior. (3, 4, 10, 11)
8. Identify historic and current sources for the pattern of rebellious actions. (4, 7)
9. Verbalize an awareness of honest feelings about rules, limits, and boundaries. (5, 10, 11)

THERAPEUTIC INTERVENTIONS

1. Assign client to read unit rules twice and summarize them to therapist.
2. Assign appropriate natural consequences when client fails to follow rules or expectations.
3. Confront client when rude or not being respectful of others and their boundaries.
4. Process with client the sources of defiant, rebellious actions.
5. Confront client when making blaming statements or failing to take responsibility for actions, thoughts, or feelings.
6. Ask support staff to redirect client when not following rules.
7. Explore with client reasons for blaming others for own actions.
8. Give verbal positive feedback to client when he/she is complying with rules without reminders and taking responsibility for his/her own behavior.
9. Attempt to sensitize client to his/her lack of empathy for others by revisiting consequences of behavior on others. Use role reversal techniques.

The numbers in parenthesis accompanying the short-term objectives correspond to the list of suggested therapeutic interventions.

—. _____
    _____
—. _____
    _____
—. _____
    _____

10. Ask client to make a list of behaviors and attitudes that must be modified in order to decrease his/her conflict with authorities. Process list with therapist.

11. Assist client to recognize and honestly express feelings related to limits, rules, and structure.

—. _____
    _____
—. _____
    _____
—. _____
    _____

DIAGNOSTIC SUGGESTIONS

Axis I:	303.90	Alcohol Dependence
	304.20	Cocaine Dependence
	304.80	Polysubstance Dependence
	309.3	Adjustment Disorder with Disturbance of Conduct
	312.81	Conduct Disorder/Childhood-Onset Type
	312.82	Conduct Disorder/Adolescent-Onset Type
	312.34	Intermittent Explosive Disorder
	_____	_____
	_____	_____
Axis II:	301.7	Antisocial Personality Disorder
	301.81	Narcissistic Personality Disorder
	_____	_____
	_____	_____

ANXIETY

BEHAVIORAL DEFINITIONS

1. Excessive anxiety and worry about several life circumstances that have no factual or logical basis. This anxiety and worry persists on a daily basis.
2. Symptoms of motor tension such as restlessness, tiredness, shakiness, or muscle tension.
3. Symptoms of autonomic hyperactivity such as palpitations, shortness of breath, dry mouth, trouble swallowing, nausea, or diarrhea.
4. Symptoms of hypervigilance such as feeling constantly on edge, concentration difficulties, trouble falling or staying asleep, and general state of irritability.

—. _____
   _____

—. _____
   _____

—. _____
   _____

LONG-TERM GOALS

1. Reduce overall level, frequency, and intensity of the anxiety so that daily functioning is not impaired.
2. Stabilize anxiety level while increasing ability to function on a daily basis.
3. Resolve the core conflict that is the source of anxiety.

—. _____
   _____

—. _____

   _____

—. _____

   _____

SHORT-TERM OBJECTIVES

1. Develop behavioral and cognitive strategies to reduce or eliminate the irrational anxiety. (1, 7, 9, 12)

2. Identify major life conflicts. (4, 10, 11)

3. Increase understanding of beliefs and messages that produce the worry and anxiety. (1, 10, 11)

4. Complete physician evaluation for medications. (2, 3)

5. Take medications as prescribed and report any side effects to appropriate professionals. (3)

6. Decrease daily level of anxiety by developing positive coping mechanisms. (1, 5, 7, 12)

7. Increase daily social and vocational involvement. (7, 8, 9)

8. Identify verbally how worries are irrational. (8, 10)

THERAPEUTIC INTERVENTIONS

1. Explore cognitive messages that mediate anxiety response and retrain in adaptive cognitions.

2. Assist in making a referral to a physician for a medication consultation.

3. Monitor medication compliance and effectiveness. Confer with physician regularly.

4. Reinforce insights into past emotional issues and present anxiety.

5. Train in guided imagery for anxiety relief.

6. Utilize biofeedback techniques to facilitate relaxation skills.

7. Assist client in developing coping strategies (e.g., increased social involvement, obtaining employment, physical exercise) for his/her anxiety.

8. Assist client in developing an awareness of the irrational nature of his/her fears.

The numbers in parentheses accompanying the short-term objectives correspond to the list of suggested therapeutic interventions.

9. Develop appropriate relaxation and diversion activities to decrease level of anxiety. (6, 7)

10. Follow through completely with the given brief solution, strategic intervention, or order developed by the therapist to decrease the anxiety. (1, 5, 10, 11)

—. _____
   _____

—. _____
   _____

—. _____
   _____

9. Help client develop reality-based cognitive messages that will increase self-confidence in coping with irrational fears.

10. Ask client to develop and process a list of key past and present life conflicts.

11. Assist client in becoming aware of key unresolved life conflicts and in starting to work toward their resolution.

12. Help client develop healthy self-talk as a means of handling the anxiety.

—. _____
   _____

—. _____
   _____

—. _____
   _____

DIAGNOSTIC SUGGESTIONS

Axis I: 300.02   Generalized Anxiety Disorder
              300.00   Anxiety Disorder NOS
              309.24   Adjustment Disorder with Anxiety

              _____   _____
              _____   _____

CHEMICAL DEPENDENCE

BEHAVIORAL DEFINITIONS

1. Consistent use of alcohol or other mood-altering drugs until high, intoxicated, or passed out.
2. Inability to stop or cut down use of mood-altering drug once started, despite the verbalized desire to do so and the negative consequences continued use brings.
3. Blood work that reflects the results of a pattern of heavy substance use, for example, elevated liver enzymes.
4. Denial that chemical dependence is a problem (e.g., "I only have a couple drinks"; "I use only on weekends"; "It's their problem, not mine") despite direct feedback from spouse, relatives, friends, and employers that the use of the substance is negatively affecting them and others.
5. Frequent blackouts when using.
6. Continued drug and/or alcohol use despite knowledge of experiencing persistent or recurring physical, legal, vocational, social, or relationship problems that are directly caused by the use of the substance.
7. Increased tolerance for the drug as there is the need to use more to become intoxicated or to recall the desired effect.
8. Physical withdrawal symptoms, that is, shaking, seizures, nausea, headaches, sweating, anxiety, insomnia, and/or depression, when going without the substance for any length of time.
9. Suspension of important social, recreational, or occupational activities because they interfere with using.
10. Large time investment in activities to obtain the substance, to use it, or to recover from its effects.
11. Consumption of substance in greater amounts and for longer periods than intended.
12. Continued use of mood-altering chemical after being told by a physician that using is causing health problems.

—. _____
    _____
—. _____
    _____

LONG-TERM GOALS

1. Accept chemical dependence and begin to actively participate in a recovery program.
2. Establish a sustained recovery, free from the use of all mood-altering substances.
3. Establish and maintain total abstinence while increasing knowledge of the disease and the process of recovery.
4. Acquire the necessary skills to maintain long-term sobriety from all mood-altering substances and live a life free of chemicals.
5. Improve quality of life by maintaining an ongoing abstinence from all mood-altering chemicals.
6. Withdraw from mood-altering substance, stabilize physically and emotionally, and then establish a supportive recovery plan.

—. _____
    _____
—. _____
    _____
—. _____
    _____

SHORT-TERM OBJECTIVES

1. Identify the negative ways using has impacted life. (1, 5, 6, 7, 9, 10)

2. Make verbal "I" statements that reflect acknowledgment and acceptance of chemical dependence. (7, 11)

3. Decrease the level of denial around using as evidenced by fewer statements about minimizing amount of use and its negative impact on life. (7, 11)

4. Verbalize increased knowledge of the disease and the process of recovery. (8, 11, 13, 17)

5. Identify the ways being sober could positively impact life. (12, 17, 23)

6. Identify potential relapse triggers and develop strategies for constructively dealing with each trigger. (11, 13, 14)

7. State key life changes necessary for sobriety in addition to not using. (11, 14, 20)

8. Identify sources of ongoing support in maintaining sobriety. (11, 16, 17, 19)

THERAPEUTIC INTERVENTIONS

1. Gather a complete drug/ alcohol history including amount and pattern of use, signs and symptoms of use, and negative life consequences (social, legal, familial, vocational) resulting from client's chemical dependence.

2. Assess client's intellectual, personality, and cognitive functioning as to his/her contribution to chemical dependence.

3. Probe client's family history for chemical dependence patterns and relate these to client's use.

4. Investigate situational stress factors that may foster client's chemical dependence.

5. Refer client for thorough physical examination to determine any physical effects of chemical dependence.

6. Ask client to make a list of the ways substance abuse has negatively impacted his/her life and process it with therapist.

The numbers in parentheses accompanying the short-term objectives correspond to the list of suggested therapeutic interventions.

9. Develop a written aftercare plan that will support the maintenance of long-term sobriety. (13, 14, 15, 17, 18)

10. Verbalize how living situation contributes to chemical dependence and acts as a hindrance to recovery. (4, 13, 14, 20, 21)

11. State the need for more stable, healthy living situation that will support recovery. (13, 14, 21, 22)

12. Make arrangements to terminate current living situation and move to a place more conducive to recovery. (15, 22)

13. Verbalize an understanding of personality, social, and family factors that foster chemical dependence. (2, 3, 4)

—. _____
   _____

—. _____
   _____

—. _____
   _____

7. Assign client to complete a First Step paper and then process it with either group, sponsor, or therapist to receive feedback.

8. Assign client to read article/ pamphlet on the disease concept of alcoholism and select several key ideas to discuss with therapist.

9. Administer the Alcohol Severity Index, and process the results with the client.

10. Assign client to ask two or three people who are close to him/her to write a letter to therapist in which they identify how they saw client's chemical dependence negatively impacting his/her life.

11. Require client to attend didactic lectures related to chemical dependence and the process of recovery. Then ask client to identify in writing several key points attained from each lecture for further processing with therapist.

12. Direct client to write a goodbye letter to drug of choice; read it and process related feelings with therapist.

13. Help client develop an awareness of relapse triggers and alternative ways of effectively handling them.

14. Assist the client in developing insight into life changes needed in order to maintain long-term sobriety.

15. Assign and review client's written aftercare plan to ensure it is adequate to maintain sobriety.

16. Recommend client attend Alcoholics Anonymous (AA) or Narcotics Anonymous (NA) meetings and report to therapist the impact of the meetings.

17. Assign client to meet with an AA/NA member who has been working the Twelve-Step program for several years and find out specifically how the program has helped him/her stay sober. Afterward, process the meeting with therapist.

18. Develop an abstinence contract with client regarding the use of his/her drug of choice. Then process the emotional impact of this contract with therapist.

19. Explore with client the positive support system personally available in sobriety and discuss ways to develop and reinforce a positive support system.

20. Evaluate the role of client's living situation in fostering pattern of chemical dependence.

21. Assign client to write a list of negative influences for chemical dependence inherent in current living situation.

22. Encourage and assist client in finding a more positive, stable living arrangement that will be supportive of recovery.

23. Ask client to make and process a list of how being sober could positively impact life.

—. _____

_____

_____

_____

—. _____

_____

_____

DIAGNOSTIC SUGGESTIONS

Axis I:	303.90	Alcohol Dependence
	305.00	Alcohol Abuse
	304.30	Cannabis Dependence
	305.20	Cannabis Abuse
	304.20	Cocaine Dependence
	305.60	Cocaine Abuse
	304.80	Polysubstance Dependence
	291.2	Alcohol-Induced Persisting Dementia
	291.1	Alcohol-Induced Persisting Amnestic Disorder
	V71.01	Adult Antisocial Behavior
	300.4	Dysthymic Disorder
	312.34	Intermittent Explosive Disorder
	309.81	Posttraumatic Stress Disorder
	304.10	Sedative, Hypnotic, or Anxiolytic Dependence
	_____	_____
	_____	_____
Axis II:	301.7	Antisocial Personality Disorder
	_____	_____
	_____	_____

CHEMICAL DEPENDENCE— RELAPSE

BEHAVIORAL DEFINITIONS

1. Inability to remain abstinent from mood-altering drugs after receiving treatment for substance abuse.
2. Inability to stay sober even though attending Alcoholics Anonymous (AA) meetings regularly.
3. Relapse into abuse of mood-altering substances after a substantial period of sobriety.

—. _____
_____

—. _____
_____

—. _____
_____

LONG-TERM GOALS

1. Reestablish an alcohol/drug–free lifestyle.
2. Develop an understanding of personal pattern of relapse in order to help sustain long-term recovery.
3. Develop an increased awareness of physical relapse triggers and the coping strategies needed to effectively deal with them.

—. _____
_____

—. _____

   _____

   _____

—. _____

   _____

SHORT-TERM OBJECTIVES

1. Verbally discuss the specific behaviors, attitudes, and feelings that led up to the last relapse, focusing on triggers for the relapse. (1, 2, 6)

2. Identify behavior patterns that will need to be changed if client is to maintain sobriety. (2, 5, 10)

3. Recall the number of relapses in the past years focusing on patterns or similarities in stresses and feeling states. (1, 2, 6, 7)

4. Verbally describe understanding of the role played by family and relationship stress in triggering relapse. (7, 10)

5. Demonstrate the ability to tolerate uncomfortable emotions that arise in group and individual sessions. (4, 5, 7)

THERAPEUTIC INTERVENTIONS

1. Ask client to develop a list of behaviors, attitudes, and feelings that could have been involved in the relapse and process it with therapist.

2. Assign client to complete a relapse workbook (e.g., *The Staying Sober Workbook* by Gorski) and process it with therapist.

3. Assign client to read a book or pamphlet on recovery. Select items from it that relate to him/her and process them with therapist.

4. Assist client in developing assertiveness techniques.

5. Work with client in group and/or individual sessions to increase understanding and tolerance of strong emotions.

The numbers in parentheses accompanying the short-term objectives correspond to the list of suggested therapeutic interventions.

7. Articulate in writing a plan of action for coping with uncomfortable feelings with steps up to and including contacting a sponsor. (8, 11)

8. Develop written continuing aftercare plan with focus on coping with family and other stressors. (8, 12)

9. Identify specific relapse triggers and develop in writing two possible coping strategies for each. (4, 5, 10)

10. Describe positive rewards associated with abstinence. (3, 9, 13)

11. Reestablish ongoing relationships with people who are supportive of sobriety. (9)

12. Articulate people and places that must be avoided to maintain recovery. (1, 2, 10)

—. _____
   _____

—. _____
   _____

—. _____
   _____

6. Ask client to gather from significant other an observation list of client's behavior or attitude prior to his/her returning to using. Process feedback in group therapy or in individual session.

7. Assign client to do a focused autobiography from first attempt to get sober to present. Then read it for feedback as to triggers for relapse.

8. Ask client to complete and process a relapse contract with significant other that identifies previous relapse-associated behaviors, attitudes, and emotions, coupling them with agreed upon warnings from significant other as they are observed.

9. Work with client to assist in reuniting with AA sponsor.

10. Assist client in identifying the negative influence of people or situations that encourage relapse and ways to avoid them.

11. Ask client to develop a list of ways to handle uncomfortable feelings and process list with therapist.

12. Assign client to develop and process a written aftercare plan that addresses specific relapse triggers previously identified.

13. Assist client in identifying
     positive rewards of total
     abstinence.

___. _____

     _____

___. _____

     _____

___. _____

     _____

DIAGNOSTIC SUGGESTIONS

Axis I: 303.90   Alcohol Dependence
              305.00   Alcohol Abuse
              304.30   Cannabis Dependence
              304.20   Cocaine Dependence
              304.80   Polysubstance Dependence
              291.1   Alcohol-Induced Persisting Amnestic Disorder
              291.2   Alcohol-Induced Persisting Dementia
              300.4   Dysthymic Disorder
              309.81   Postraumatic Stress Disorder

_____   _____

_____   _____

Axis II: 301.7   Antisocial Personality Disorder

_____   _____

_____   _____

CHILDHOOD TRAUMAS

BEHAVIORAL DEFINITIONS

1. Reports of childhood physical, sexual, or emotional abuse.
2. Description of parents as physically or emotionally neglectful as they were chemically dependent, too busy, absent, and so on.
3. Description of childhood as chaotic as parent(s) was substance abuser (or mentally ill, antisocial, etc.), leading to frequent moves, multiple abusive spousal partners, frequent substitute caretakers, financial pressures, and/or many step-siblings.
4. Reports of emotionally repressive parents who were rigid, perfectionistic, threatening, demeaning, hypercritical, and/or hyperreligious.
5. Irrational fears, suppressed rage, low self-esteem, identity conflicts, depression, or anxious insecurity related to painful early life experiences.
6. Dissociative phenomena (multiple personality, psychogenic fugue or amnesia, trance state, and/or depersonalization) evidenced in behavior as maladaptive coping mechanisms resulting from childhood emotional pain.

—. _____

_____

—. _____

_____

—. _____

_____

LONG-TERM GOALS

1. Develop an awareness of how childhood issues have affected and continue to affect one's family life.
2. Resolve past childhood/family issues leading to less anger and depression, greater self-esteem, security, and confidence.
3. Release the emotions associated with past childhood/family issues resulting in less resentment and more serenity.
4. Let go of blame and begin to forgive others for pain caused in childhood.

—. _____

_____

—. _____

_____

—. _____

_____

SHORT-TERM OBJECTIVES

1. Describe what it was like to grow up in client's family. (1, 2, 3)

2. Identify the role played within the family and feelings associated with that role. (1, 2, 4)

3. Increase awareness of how client's upbringing has affected him/her emotionally and behaviorally. (3, 4, 5)

4. Identify feelings associated with parental child-rearing patterns. (2, 6)

THERAPEUTIC INTERVENTIONS

1. Explore family-related issues to increase openness and understanding.

2. Develop client's family genogram and/or symptom line and help identify patterns within the family.

3. Support and encourage client when he/she begins to express feelings of rage, fear, and rejection relating to family abuse or neglect.

4. Ask client to read the books *It Will Never Happen to Me* (Black); *Outgrowing the Pain* (Gil); *Healing the*

The numbers in parentheses accompanying the short-term objectives correspond to the list of suggested therapeutic interventions.

5. Identify feelings associated with major traumatic incidents in childhood. (3, 4, 5)

6. Increase understanding and awareness of the effect of how client was parented has on the way he/she parents his/her children. (2, 4, 6)

7. Decrease blame regarding childhood issues and increase ownership of feelings. (4, 7, 8)

8. Identify patterns within the family of origin both current and historical, nuclear and extended. (1, 2, 4, 6)

9. Verbally show recognition between beginning of substance abuse and family conflict. (1, 2, 3, 4)

10. State the role substance abuse has in dealing with emotional pain of childhood. (1, 2, 3, 4)

11. Express a desire to begin process of forgiveness of others for the pain of childhood. (4, 5, 8)

12. Demonstrate awareness of and control over actions initiated by various identities. (9, 10)

—. _____
   _____

—. _____
   _____

—. _____
   _____

Child Within (Whitfield); *Why I'm Afraid to Tell You Who I Am* (Powell); and identify insights attained.

5. Assign feelings journal that shows the memories and emotions tied to traumatic childhood experiences.

6. Assign asking parents about *their* family backgrounds and develop insight regarding patterns of behavior and causes for parents' dysfunction.

7. Assign writing a letter to mother, father, or whomever in which the client expresses his/her feelings regarding childhood trauma.

8. Encourage client to release hurt and anger in order to begin process of forgiveness and development of self-esteem.

9. Assess the severity of dissociation phenomena occurring and hospitalize as necessary for client protection.

10. Assist client in understanding the role of dissociation in protecting self from pain of childhood abusive betrayals.

—. _____
   _____

—. _____
   _____

—. _____
   _____

DIAGNOSTIC SUGGESTIONS

Axis I:

300.4	Dysthymic Disorder
296.xx	Major Depressive Disorder
300.3	Obsessive-Compulsive Disorder
300.02	Generalized Anxiety Disorder
309.81	Posttraumatic Stress Disorder
300.14	Dissociative Identity Disorder
V61.21	Sexual Abuse of Child (995.53, Victim)
V61.21	Physical Abuse of Child (995.54, Victim)
V61.21	Neglect of Child (995.52, Victim)
_____	_____
_____	_____

Axis II:

301.7	Antisocial Personality Disorder
301.6	Dependent Personality Disorder
301.4	Obsessive-Compulsive Personality Disorder
_____	_____
_____	_____

COGNITIVE DEFICITS

BEHAVIORAL DEFINITIONS

1. Concrete thinking or impaired abstract thinking.
2. Lack of insight into the consequences of behavior or impaired judgment.
3. Short-term or long-term memory deficits.
4. Difficulty following complex directions.
5. Loss of orientation to time, person, or place.
6. Distractibility in attention.

___. _____

_____

_____

___. _____

_____

_____

___. _____

_____

LONG-TERM GOALS

1. Determine the degree of cognitive impairment.
2. Develop alternative coping strategies to compensate for cognitive limitations.

___. _____

_____

_____

___. _____

_____

_____

___. _____

_____

SHORT-TERM OBJECTIVES

1. Cooperate with and complete organicity testing. (1, 2)

2. Increase basic understanding of cause and effect relationships. (3, 7)

3. Implement memory-enhancing mechanisms. (6, 8)

4. Demonstrate the ability to follow through to completion of simple tasks. (6)

5. Identify when it is appropriate to seek help with a task and when it is not. (5, 6, 9)

6. Understand and accept cognitive limitations and use alternate coping mechanisms. (3, 8, 9, 10)

—. _____
_____

—. _____
_____

—. _____
_____

THERAPEUTIC INTERVENTIONS

1. Refer and arrange for client to have psychological testing to determine nature and degree of cognitive deficits.

2. Administer appropriate psychological tests (e.g., Wechsler Adult Intelligence Scale—Revised, Booklet Category Test, Trailmaking, Halstead-Reitan Battery, Michigan Neurological Battery, Luria-Nebraska Battery, Wechsler Memory Scale, Memory Assessment Scales) to determine nature and extent of cognitive deficits.

3. Discuss results of testing with psychologist and develop appropriate objectives based on testing.

4. Refer to neurologist, if appropriate, to further assess organic deficits and possible causes.

5. Assess and monitor cognitive behavior in individual sessions.

6. Assign appropriate tasks for client to follow through on and redirect when needed so as to assess cognitive abilities.

7. Discuss in individual therapy sessions cause and effect relationships.

The numbers in parentheses accompanying the short-term objectives correspond to the list of suggested therapeutic interventions.

8. Assign and monitor memory-enhancing activities/exercises and memory-loss coping strategies such as lists, routines, and the like.

9. Establish with client and significant other appropriate points for client to ask for help.

10. Assist client in coming to an understanding and acceptance of limitations.

___. _____

_____

___. _____

_____

___. _____

_____

DIAGNOSTIC SUGGESTIONS

Axis I:	310.1	Personality Change Due to (Axis III Disorder)
	294.8	Dementia NOS
	294.1	Dementia Due to (Axis III Disorder)
	291.2	Alcohol-Induced Persisting Dementia
	291.1	Alcohol-Induced Persisting Amnestic Disorder
	294.8	Amnestic Disorder NOS
	303.90	Alcohol Dependence
	304.30	Cannabis Dependence
	294.0	Amnestic Disorder Due to (Axis III Disorder)
	294.9	Cognitive Disorder NOS
	_____	_____
	_____	_____

DEPENDENCY

BEHAVIORAL DEFINITIONS

1. All feelings of self-worth, happiness, and fulfillment derive from relationships.
2. Involvement in at least two relationships in which he/she was physically abused but had difficulty leaving.
3. A history of multi-intimate relationships with little if any space between the ending of one and the start of the next.
4. Strong feelings of panic, fear, and helplessness when faced with being alone as a close relationship ends.
5. Inability to become self-sufficient, consistently allowing or falling back on parents to provide financial support, housing, or caregiving.
6. Susceptibility to feeling hurt by criticism.
7. Incapacity to make important decisions.
8. Avoidance, at great lengths, of being alone.
9. Frequent preoccupation with fears of being abandoned.
10. Inability to disagree with others for fear of being rejected.
11. Inability to make decisions or initiate action without excessive reassurance from others.

—. _____

_____

—. _____

_____

—. _____

_____

LONG-TERM GOALS

1. Begin the development of an independent self that is able to meet some of his/her needs and to tolerate being alone.
2. Achieve a balance between healthy independence and healthy dependence.
3. Decrease dependence on relationships while beginning to meet his/her own needs, build confidence, and practice assertiveness.
4. Establish firm individual self-boundaries and improved self-worth.

—. _____

_____

_____

—. _____

_____

_____

—. _____

_____

SHORT-TERM OBJECTIVES

1. Develop the ability to verbally state his/her opinion. (2, 3, 5, 6)
2. Decrease the automatic practice of meeting other people's expectations. (3, 4, 5, 6)
3. Increase saying no to others' requests. (3, 5, 6, 15, 22)
4. Identify and clarify own emotional and social needs. (1, 6, 10, 21)
5. Increase ability to fulfill own needs. (1, 6, 10, 16)

THERAPEUTIC INTERVENTIONS

1. Ask client to put together a list of needs and ways that these could be possibly be met. Process list with therapist.
2. Assign client to speak his/her mind for one day and process the results with therapist.
3. Assign client to say no without excessive explanation for a period of one week and process this with therapist.
4. Ask client to make a thorough list of "musts" and "shoulds" and process it with therapist.

_____

The numbers in parentheses accompanying the short-term objectives correspond to the list of suggested therapeutic interventions.

6. Develop a clear-cut set of limits for self and not take responsibility for others' behavior and feelings. (5, 6, 13)

7. Increase sense of personal empowerment. (3, 5, 7, 20)

8. Decrease sensitivity to criticism. (5, 7, 18, 20)

9. Increase knowledge of healthy dependency and healthy independence. (5, 6, 8, 10)

10. Identify healthy ways to increase independence. (9, 14, 17, 22)

11. Increase sense of self-responsibility while decreasing sense of responsibility for others. (5, 6, 15, 17)

12. Identify and set new boundaries for self in key life relationships. (11, 12, 13)

13. Increase awareness of boundaries and when they are violated. (8, 11, 13)

14. Develop the ability to verbally clarify boundaries with others. (8, 13, 17, 19)

15. Increase ability to allow others to do things for him/ her and to receive without giving. (6, 10, 16)

16. Increase ability to say no without feelings of guilt. (3, 5, 6, 22)

__. _____

_____

5. Refer to assertiveness-training classes.

6. Refer to Alanon or another appropriate self-help group.

7. Assign client to institute a ritual of beginning each day with 5–10 minutes of solitude where the focus is personal affirmation.

8. Assist client in developing new boundaries that support healthy independence.

9. Explore and clarify fears or other feelings associated with being more independent.

10. Assign client to read the books *Codependent No More* (Beattie); *Women Who Love Too Much* (Norwood); *Getting Them Sober* (Drews); and process key ideas with therapist.

11. Assign client to read the book *Boundaries and Relationships* (Whitfield) and process key ideas with therapist.

12. Ask client to read the chapter on setting boundaries and limits in the book *A Gift to Myself* (Whitfield) and complete the survey on personal boundaries that is part of the chapter. Process key ideas and results of survey with therapist.

13. Assist the client in developing new ways to set and implement boundaries and limits for self.

___. _____

  _____

___. _____

  _____

14. Facilitate conjoint session with significant other with focus on exploring ways to increase independence within the relationship.

15. Develop a family genogram to increase client's awareness of family patterns of dependence in relationships and how he/she is repeating them in the present relationship.

16. Assign client to allow others to do for him/her and to receive without giving. Report progress and feelings related to this assignment to therapist.

17. Assist client in identifying and implementing ways of increasing his/her level of independence in day-to-day life.

18. Explore client's sensitivity to criticism and help develop new ways of receiving, processing, and responding to it.

19. Verbally reinforce any and all signs of assertiveness and independence.

20. Confront client's decision avoidance and encourage decision-making process.

21. Explore family of origin for experiences of emotional abandonment.

22. Explore client's automatic thoughts associated with assertiveness, being alone, or not meeting others' needs.

—. _____

_____

—. _____

_____

—. _____

_____

DIAGNOSTIC SUGGESTIONS

Axis I: 300.4   Dysthymic Disorder
V61.12   Physical Abuse of Adult by Partner (995.81, Victim)
V62.83   Physical Abuse of Adult by Person Other than Partner
(995.81, Victim)

_____   _____

_____   _____

Axis II: 301.82   Avoidant Personality Disorder
301.83   Borderline Personality Disorder
301.6   Dependent Personality Disorder

_____   _____

_____   _____

DEPRESSION

BEHAVIORAL DEFINITIONS

1. Loss of appetite.
2. Depressed affect.
3. Diminished interest in or enjoyment of activities.
4. Psychomotor agitation or retardation.
5. Sleeplessness or hypersomnia.
6. Lack of energy.
7. Poor concentration and indecisiveness.
8. Social withdrawal.
9. Suicidal thoughts and/or gestures.
10. Feelings of hopelessness, worthlessness, or inappropriate guilt.
11. Low self-esteem.
12. Unresolved grief issues.
13. Mood-related hallucinations or delusions.
14. History of chronic or recurrent depression for which client has taken antidepressant medication, been hospitalized, had outpatient treatment or a course of electroconvulsive therapy.

—. _____
   _____

—. _____
   _____

—. _____
   _____

LONG-TERM GOALS

1. Appropriately grieve the loss of spouse in order to normalize mood and to return to previous adaptive level of functioning.

2. Develop the ability to recognize, accept, and cope with feelings of depression.
3. Alleviate depressed mood and return to previous level of effective functioning.
4. Develop healthy cognitive patterns and beliefs about self and the world that lead to alleviation of depression symptoms.

—. _____

_____

—. _____

_____

—. _____

_____

SHORT-TERM OBJECTIVES

1. Verbally identify, if possible, the source of depressed mood. (1, 4)
2. Discuss the nature of the relationship with deceased significant other, reminiscing about time spent together. (4, 5)
3. Discuss overreliance on significant other for support, direction, and meaning to life. (4, 5, 13)
4. Report on awareness of anger toward spouse/ significant other for leaving. (1, 4, 5, 13)
5. Verbalize an understanding of the relationship between repressed anger and depressed mood. (4, 6, 11)

THERAPEUTIC INTERVENTIONS

1. Ask client to make a list of what he/she is depressed about and process list with therapist.
2. Assess need for antidepressant medication and arrange for prescription, if appropriate.
3. Monitor and evaluate medication compliance and the effectiveness of the medications on level of functioning.
4. Encourage sharing feelings of depression in order to clarify them and gain insight as to causes.

The numbers in parentheses accompanying the short-term objectives correspond to the list of suggested therapeutic interventions.

6. Begin to experience sadness in session while discussing the disappointment related to the loss or pain from the past. (4, 5)

7. Verbally express understanding of the relationship between depressed mood and repression of feelings—that is, anger, hurt, sadness, and so on. (12)

8. Take prescribed medications responsibly at times ordered by physician. (2, 3)

9. Report to appropriate professional any side effects experienced from the medications. (3)

10. Complete Minnesota Multiphasic Personality Inventory (MMPI), Beck Depression Inventory (BDI), or other psychological testing to determine level of depression and need for medication (i.e., antidepressant) or suicide precaution measures. (2, 9, 15, 16)

11. Show evidence of daily care for personal grooming and hygiene with minimal reminders from others. (10)

12. Identify cognitive self-talk that is engaged in to support depression. (12, 13)

13. Replace negative and self-defeating self-talk with verbalization of realistic and positive cognitive messages. (6, 8, 14)

5. Ask client to write a letter to lost loved one regarding feelings of loss, anger, guilt, and so forth, and share that letter to receive feedback.

6. Assign chemically dependent client to read passages related to depression from the books *One Day at a Time* (Hallinan) and *Each Day a New Beginning* (Hazelden Staff).

7. Assign participation in recreational activities.

8. Assign client to write at least one positive affirmation statement daily regarding himself/herself.

9. Arrange administration of MMPI and/or BDI and evaluate the results.

10. Monitor and redirect client on daily grooming and hygiene.

11. Assist in developing coping strategies (e.g., more physical exercise, less internal focus, increased social involvement, more assertiveness, greater need sharing, more anger expression) for feelings of depression.

12. Assist in teaching more about depression and accepting some sadness as a normal variation in feeling.

13. Assist in developing awareness of cognitive messages that reinforce hopelessness and helplessness.

14. State he/she no longer has thoughts of self-harm. (15, 16)

15. Verbalize hopeful and positive statements regarding the future. (8, 13, 14)

16. Make positive statements regarding self and ability to cope with stresses of life. (8, 14)

17. Engage in physical and recreational activities that reflect increased energy and interest. (7, 11)

18. Participate in social contacts and initiate communication of needs and desires. (11, 17)

__. _____

_____

__. _____

_____

__. _____

_____

14. Reinforce positive, reality-based cognitive messages that enhance self-confidence and increase adaptive action.

15. Assess and monitor suicide potential.

16. Arrange for hospitalization, as necessary, when client is judged to be harmful to self.

17. Reinforce social activities and verbalization of feelings, needs, and desires.

__. _____

_____

__. _____

_____

__. _____

_____

DIAGNOSTIC SUGGESTIONS

Axis I:

309.0	Adjustment Disorder with Depressed Mood
296.xx	Bipolar I Disorder
296.89	Bipolar II Disorder
300.4	Dysthymic Disorder
301.13	Cyclothymic Disorder
296.2x	Major Depressive Disorder Single Episode
296.3x	Major Depressive Disorder, Recurrent
295.70	Schizoaffective Disorder
310.1	Personality Change Due to (Axis III Disorder)
V62.82	Bereavement
_____	_____
_____	_____

DISSOCIATION

BEHAVIORAL DEFINITIONS

1. The existence within the person of two or more distinct personalities or personality-states that recurrently take full control of the person's behavior.
2. An episode of sudden inability to remember important personal information that is more than just ordinary forgetfulness.
3. Persistent or recurrent experiences of depersonalization, like feeling detached from or outside of one's mental processes or body during which reality testing remains intact.
4. Persistent or recurrent experiences of depersonalization as if one is automated or in a dream.
5. Depersonalization sufficiently severe and persistent as to cause marked distress in daily life.

—. _____

_____

—. _____

_____

—. _____

_____

LONG-TERM GOALS

1. Begin the process of integrating the various personalities.
2. Reduce the frequency and duration of dissociative episodes.
3. Resolve the emotional trauma that underlies the dissociative disturbance.
4. Reduce the level of daily distress caused by dissociative disturbances.
5. Regain full memory.

—. _____
   _____
   _____

—. _____
   _____
   _____

—. _____
   _____

SHORT-TERM OBJECTIVES

1. Identify each personality and have each tell its story. (1, 9)

2. Complete a medication evaluation with a physician. (2)

3. Take prescribed medications responsibly at times ordered by physician. (3)

4. Identify key issues that trigger dissociative state. (4, 5)

5. Increase disclosure about key unresolved issues without dissociating. (6, 7, 9)

6. Discuss period preceding memory loss and period after memory returns. (4, 8, 9)

7. Increase memory of personal information or lost span of time. (4, 8, 9)

8. Decrease number and duration of personality changes. (5, 6, 7, 9)

THERAPEUTIC INTERVENTIONS

1. Probe and assess the existence of the various personalities that take control of the patient.

2. Arrange for a client to have an evaluation for medications with a physician and consult with physician on his/her conclusions.

3. Monitor and evaluate client's medication compliance and the effectiveness of the medication on the level of functioning.

4. Explore sources of emotional pain, feelings of fear, inadequacy, rejection, or abuse.

5. Assist client in acceptance of connection between dissociating and avoidance of facing emotional conflicts/issues.

The numbers in parentheses accompanying the short-term objectives correspond to the list of suggested therapeutic interventions.

—. _____
_____

—. _____
_____

—. _____
_____

6. Facilitate integration of personality by supporting and encouraging client to talk about emotional traumas without dissociating.

7. Develop and implement a reparative process for the client.

8. Arrange and facilitate a session with significant others and client to assist in regaining lost personal information.

9. Actively build level of trust with client to help increase ability to self-disclose.

—. _____
_____

—. _____
_____

—. _____
_____

DIAGNOSTIC SUGGESTIONS

Axis I:	303.90	Alcohol Dependence
	300.14	Dissociative Identity Disorder
	300.12	Dissociative Amnesia
	300.6	Depersonalization Disorder
	300.15	Dissociative Disorder NOS
	_____	_____
	_____	_____

EATING DISORDER

BEHAVIORAL DEFINITIONS

1. Rapid consumption of large quantities of food in a short time followed by self-induced vomiting and/or use of laxatives due to fear of weight gain.
2. Extreme weight loss (and amenorrhea in females) with refusal to maintain a minimal healthy weight due to very limited ingestion of food and high frequency of secretive self-induced vomiting, inappropriate use of laxatives, and/or excessive strenuous exercise.
3. Preoccupation with body image related to grossly unrealistic assessment of self as being too fat or strong denial of seeing self as emaciated.
4. An irrational fear of becoming overweight.
5. Fluid and electrolyte imbalance resulting from eating disorder.

—. _____
   _____
   _____
—. _____
   _____
   _____
—. _____
   _____

LONG-TERM GOALS

1. Restore normal eating patterns, body weight, balanced fluid and electrolytes, and realistic perception of body size.
2. Terminate pattern of binge eating and vomiting with a return to normal eating of enough nutritious foods to maintain healthy weight.

___. _____

     _____

     _____

___. _____

     _____

     _____

___. _____

     _____

SHORT-TERM OBJECTIVES

1. Cooperate with a full physical and dental exam. (1, 2)
2. Consume at least the minimal necessary daily calories to progressively gain weight. (3, 4, 5, 21)
3. Terminate inappropriate laxative use. (8, 9, 21, 22)
4. Terminate self-induced vomiting. (4, 8, 9, 21, 22)
5. Stop hoarding food. (8, 9, 10, 22)
6. Set reasonable limits on physical exercise. (8, 14, 22)
7. Verbalize a realistic appraisal of weight status and body size. (3, 13, 14, 15)
8. Gradually accept personal responsibility for adequate nutrition as evidenced by progressive weight gain or maintenance of adequate weight without supervision from others. (4, 5, 9, 11, 21)

THERAPEUTIC INTERVENTIONS

1. Refer to physician for physical exam.
2. Refer to dentist for dental exam.
3. Monitor weight and give realistic feedback regarding body thinness.
4. Establish minimal daily caloric intake.
5. Assist in meal planning.
6. Assign journal of food intake, thoughts, and feelings.
7. Process journal information.
8. Monitor vomiting frequency, food hoarding, exercise levels, and laxative usage.
9. Reinforce weight gain and acceptance of personal responsibility for normal food intake.
10. Process issue of passive-aggressive control in rebellion against authority figures.

The numbers in parentheses accompanying the short-term objectives correspond to the list of suggested therapeutic interventions.

9. Attain and maintain balanced fluids and electrolytes as well as resumption of reproductive functions. (4, 5, 12, 21)

10. Discuss the role of passive-aggressive control in the avoidance of eating. (10, 18)

11. Discuss the role of fear of sexual identity and development in severe weight loss. (12, 13, 16)

12. Identify irrational beliefs regarding eating normal amounts of food. (11, 13, 14, 16)

13. Verbalize acceptance of sexual impulses and a desire for intimacy. (12, 16, 17)

14. Identify fear of failure and drive for perfectionism and probe roots for low self-esteem. (14, 15, 20)

15. Verbalize acceptance of shortcomings and normal failures as part of human condition. (14, 15, 22)

16. Discuss separation anxiety related to emancipation process. (10, 17, 20)

17. Develop assertive behaviors that allow for healthy expression of needs and emotions. (18, 19)

18. Discuss with family members feelings of fear related to separation. (17, 19, 20)

11. Discuss issues of food control as related to fear of losing control of eating.

12. Discuss fear of losing control of sexual impulses.

13. Assist in identification of negative cognitive messages that mediate avoidance of food intake.

14. Discuss fear of failure and role of perfectionism in search for control and avoidance of failure.

15. Reinforce client's positive qualities and successes to reduce fear of failure.

16. Process fears regarding sexual development and sexual impulses.

17. Discuss fears related to emancipation from parent figures.

18. Reinforce assertiveness behaviors in session and reports of successful assertiveness between sessions.

19. Train in assertiveness or refer to an assertiveness-training class.

20. Facilitate family therapy sessions that focus on owning feelings, clarifying messages, and identifying control conflicts.

21. Refer for inpatient hospitalization, as necessary, if client's weight loss becomes severe and physical health is jeopardized.

19. Discuss with family members feelings of ambivalence regarding control and dependency. (10, 14, 19, 20)

20. Keep a daily journal of activities, thoughts, and feelings, noting any association with eating behavior. (6, 7, 10, 12, 13)

—. _____

—. _____

—. _____

22. Refer to support group for eating disorders.

—. _____

—. _____

—. _____

DIAGNOSTIC SUGGESTIONS

Axis I: 307.1   Anorexia Nervosa
             307.51   Bulimia Nervosa
             307.50   Eating Disorder NOS

             _____   _____

             _____   _____

Axis II: 301.6   Dependent Personality Disorder

             _____   _____

             _____   _____

EDUCATIONAL DEFICITS

BEHAVIORAL DEFINITIONS

1. Incompletion of requirements for high school diploma or GED.
2. Possession of no marketable employment skills and need for vocational training.
3. Functional illiteracy.

—. _____
_____

—. _____
_____

—. _____
_____

LONG-TERM GOALS

1. Recognize the need for high school completion or GED and reenroll in the necessary courses.
2. Seek out vocational training to obtain marketable employment skill.
3. Increase literacy skills.

—. _____
_____

—. _____
_____

—. _____
_____

SHORT-TERM OBJECTIVES

1. Identify the negative consequences that have occurred due to lack of high school completion. (1, 5, 10)
2. Verbally verify the need for a high school diploma or GED. (1, 2, 5, 9)
3. Make the necessary contacts to investigate enrollment in high school completion or GED. (3, 4)
4. Make contact with agencies that offer vocational assessment and training. (4, 5)
5. State commitment to obtain further academic or vocational training. (5, 11)
6. Begin attendance at classes to obtain further academic or vocational training. (5, 6)
7. Agree to pursue educational assistance to attain reading skills. (5, 6, 7, 8, 11)
8. Follow through on attendance at adult education classes in reading. (6)

__. _____
   _____
__. _____
   _____
__. _____
   _____

THERAPEUTIC INTERVENTIONS

1. Confront client with the need for further education.
2. Support and direct client toward obtaining further academic training.
3. Provide client with information regarding community resources available for adult education.
4. Assign client to make preliminary contact with vocational and/or educational training agencies and report back regarding the experience.
5. Reinforce and encourage client in pursuing educational and/or vocational training by pointing out the social, monetary, and self-esteem advantages.
6. Monitor and support attendance at educational or vocational classes.
7. Assess the client's reading deficits.
8. Assist client in finding necessary resources that provide education in reading.
9. Facilitate client openness regarding shame or embarrassment surrounding lack of reading ability, educational achievement, or vocational skill.

The numbers in parentheses accompanying the short-term objectives correspond to the list of suggested therapeutic interventions.

10. Assist client in listing the negative effects that the lack of a GED or high school diploma has had on his/her life.

11. Obtain a verbal commitment to pursue high school completion courses, vocational training, a GED, or reading literacy education.

__. _____

_____

__. _____

_____

__. _____

_____

DIAGNOSTIC SUGGESTIONS

Axis I: V62.3   Academic Problem
V62.2   Occupational Problem
315.2   Disorder of Written Expression
315.00   Reading Disorder

_____   _____

_____   _____

Axis II: V62.89   Borderline Intellectual Functioning
317   Mild Mental Retardation

_____   _____

_____   _____

FAMILY CONFLICTS

BEHAVIORAL DEFINITIONS

1. Constant or frequent conflict with parents and/or siblings.
2. A family that is not a stable source of positive influence or support since family members have little or no contact with each other.
3. Ongoing conflict between client and parents, which is characterized by parents fostering dependence and client feeling that parents are overly involved in client's life.
4. Residence with parents and inability to live independently for more than a brief period.
5. Long periods of noncommunication with parents, and description of self as the "black sheep."

—. _____
_____
—. _____
_____
—. _____
_____

LONG-TERM GOALS

1. Resolve fear of rejection, low self-esteem, and/or oppositional defiance by understanding and resolving conflicts developed in the family of origin and their connection to current life.
2. Begin the process of emancipating from parents in a healthy way by making arrangements for independent living.
3. Decrease the level of present conflict with parents while beginning to let go of or resolving past conflicts with them.

—. _____
   _____
—. _____
   _____

SHORT-TERM OBJECTIVES

1. Describe the conflicts and understand the causes of the conflicts between self and parents. (1, 5)

2. Identify own role in the family conflicts. (1, 3, 5)

3. Identify factors that keep client dependent on the family and discover how to overcome them. (2, 3, 4, 7)

4. Increase awareness of the family dynamics and how the family system reinforces the status quo. (6, 8)

5. Verbally describe his/her understanding of the role played by family relationship stress in triggering substance abuse or relapse. (1, 2, 7, 8)

6. Increase level of independent functioning—that is, finding and keeping a job, saving money, socializing with friends, finding own housing, and so on. (2, 6, 7, 8)

THERAPEUTIC INTERVENTIONS

1. Process conflicts and causes with client in individual therapy sessions.

2. Ask client to make a list of ways he/she is dependent on parents. Process list with therapist.

3. Ask client to read the book *Making Peace with Your Parents* (Bloomfield and Felder) and select concepts from it to begin using in conflict resolution.

4. Give verbal permission for client to have and express own feelings, thoughts, and perspectives in order to foster a sense of autonomy from family.

5. Confront client when he/she is not taking responsibility for self in family conflict.

6. Conduct family therapy sessions with client and parents to facilitate healthy communication, conflict resolution, and emancipation process.

_____

The numbers in parentheses accompanying the short-term objectives correspond to the list of suggested therapeutic interventions.

7. Increase the number of positive family interactions by planning activities such as bowling, fishing, playing table games, or doing work projects. (6, 9)

8. Decrease the number and frequency of conflictual interactions with parent(s) by using "time out" to deescalate the conflict. (3, 6)

9. Increase ability to resolve conflicts with parent by talking calmly and assertively rather than aggressively and defensively. (3, 10)

10. Arrange, attend, and participate in family therapy session. (6, 10)

11. State goal and plan for emancipation. (4, 6)

—. _____
_____

—. _____
_____

—. _____
_____

7. Probe client's fears surrounding emancipation.

8. Confront emotional dependence and avoidance of economic responsibility that promotes continuing pattern of living with parents.

9. Assist family to become aware of healthy recreational activities they can become involved in together, assigning one activity each week.

10. Help client develop specific constructive ways to interact with parents.

—. _____
_____

—. _____
_____

—. _____
_____

DIAGNOSTIC SUGGESTIONS

Axis I: 300.4   Dysthymic Disorder
                300.00   Anxiety Disorder NOS
                312.34   Intermittent Explosive Disorder
                303.90   Alcohol Dependence
                304.20   Cocaine Dependence
                304.80   Polysubstance Dependence

                _____   _____

                _____   _____

Axis II: 301.7   Antisocial Personality Disorder
                301.6   Dependent Personality Disorder
                301.83   Borderline Personality Disorder
                301.9   Personality Disorder NOS

                _____   _____

                _____   _____

FEMALE SEXUAL DYSFUNCTION

BEHAVIORAL DEFINITIONS

1. Consistently very low desire for or no pleasurable anticipation of sexual activity.
2. Strong avoidance of and/or repulsion to any and all sexual contact in spite of a relationship of mutual caring and respect.
3. Recurrent lack of usual physiological response of sexual excitement and arousal (genital lubrication and swelling).
4. Consistent lack of subjective sense of enjoyment and pleasure during sexual activity.
5. Persistent delay in or absence of reaching orgasm after achieving arousal and in spite of sensitive sexual pleasuring by a caring partner.
6. Genital pain before, during, or after sexual intercourse.
7. Consistent or recurring involuntary spasm of the vagina that prohibits penetration for sexual intercourse.

—. _____

_____

—. _____

_____

—. _____

_____

LONG-TERM GOALS

1. Increase desire for and enjoyment of sexual activity.
2. Attain and maintain physiological excitement response during sexual intercourse.

3. Reach orgasm within a reasonable amount of time, intensity, and focus to sexual stimulation.
4. Eliminate pain and promote subjective pleasure before, during, and after sexual intercourse.
5. Eliminate vaginal spasms that prohibit penile penetration during sexual intercourse and achieve a sense of relaxed enjoyment of co-ital pleasure.

—. _____

 _____

—. _____

 _____

—. _____

 _____

SHORT-TERM OBJECTIVES

1. Share thoughts and feelings regarding relationship with sexual partner. (1, 2)

2. Openly discuss with partner conflicts and unfulfilled needs in the relationship that lead to anger and emotional distance. (2)

3. Discuss sexual attitudes learned in family of origin experiences. (3, 8, 9, 10)

4. Verbalize positive and healthy sexual attitudes. (1, 7, 19, 23)

5. Verbalize a resolution of feelings regarding sexual trauma or abuse experiences. (4, 5, 6)

THERAPEUTIC INTERVENTIONS

1. Assess the relationship with sexual partner as to level of harmony and fulfillment.

2. Direct conjoint sessions that focus on conflict resolution, expression of feelings, and sex education.

3. Probe family of origin history for causes of inhibition, guilt, fear, or repulsion.

4. Probe client's history for experience of sexual trauma or abuse.

5. Process emotions surrounding an emotional trauma in the sexual arena.

6. Discuss feelings regarding body image focusing on causes for negativism.

The numbers in parentheses accompanying the short-term objectives correspond to the list of suggested therapeutic interventions.

6. Describe negative feelings regarding sexual experiences of childhood or adolescence. (4, 5, 8, 9)

7. Verbalize a positive body image. (6, 7, 18)

8. State acceptance of sexual feelings and behavior as normal and healthy. (18, 19, 23)

9. Provide a detailed sexual history that explores all experiences that influence sexual attitudes, feelings, and behavior. (3, 4, 8, 9)

10. Verbalize an understanding of the role family of origin experiences have played in development of negative sexual attitudes and responses. (3, 8, 9, 10)

11. State an understanding of how religious training negatively influenced sexual thoughts, feelings, and behavior. (8, 9, 10)

12. Verbalize negative cognitive messages that trigger fears, shame, anger, or grief during sex activity. (11, 12)

13. Verbalize the development of positive and healthy automatic thoughts that mediate relaxed pleasure. (11, 12, 13, 14)

14. Practice sensate focus exercises alone and with partner and share feelings associated with activity. (13, 14, 22, 23)

7. Assign client to list assets of her body.

8. Obtain a detailed sexual history that examines current adult sexual functioning as well as childhood and adolescent experiences, level and sources of sexual knowledge, typical sexual practices and frequency of them, medical history, and use of mood-altering substances.

9. Explore role of family of origin in teaching negative attitudes regarding sexuality.

10. Explore role of religious training in reinforcing feelings of guilt and shame surrounding sexual behavior and thoughts.

11. Probe automatic thoughts that trigger negative emotions before, during, and after sexual activity.

12. Train client in healthy alternative thoughts that will mediate pleasure, relaxation, and disinhibition.

13. Give permission for less inhibited, less constricted sexual behavior by assigning body-pleasuring exercises with partner.

14. Assign body exploration and awareness exercises that reduce inhibition and desensitize client to sexual aversion.

15. Abstain from substance abuse patterns that interfere with sexual response. (8, 15)

16. Verbalize an understanding of the role physical disease or medication has on sexual dysfunction. (15, 16, 17)

17. Cooperate with a physician's complete examination and report results. (15, 16, 17)

18. Demonstrate healthy and accurate knowledge of sexuality by freely verbalizing adequate information of sexual functioning using appropriate terms for sexually related body parts. (18, 19, 23)

19. Write about sexual feelings and thoughts in a daily journal. (18, 19, 23)

20. Verbalize increasing desire for and pleasure with sexual activity. (20, 21, 22)

21. Report to therapist regarding progress on use of masturbation and vaginal dilator to achieve relaxed comfort with penetration. (14, 21, 26)

22. Practice gradual client-controlled vaginal penetration with partner. (14, 21, 22)

23. Read and discuss books assigned on human sexuality. (18, 23)

15. Assess the possible role that substance abuse, diabetes, hypertension, or thyroid disease may have on sexual functioning.

16. Review medications taken by client with regard to their possible negative side effects on sexual functioning.

17. Refer to a physician for a complete physical to rule out any organic basis for dysfunction.

18. Disinhibit and educate the client by talking freely and respectfully regarding sexual body parts, sexual feelings, and sexual behavior.

19. Assign client to keep a journal of sexual thoughts and feelings to increase awareness and acceptance of them as normal.

20. Assign graduated steps of sexual pleasuring exercises with partner that reduce performance anxiety and focus on experiencing bodily arousal sensations.

21. Direct the use of masturbation and/or vaginal dilator devices to reinforce relaxation and success surrounding vaginal penetration.

22. Direct client's sexual partner in sexual exercises that allow for client-controlled level of genital stimulation and gradually increased vaginal penetration.

24. Verbalize an understanding of the connection between lack of positive sex role model in childhood and current adult sexual dysfunction. (3, 8, 9, 24)
25. Verbalize connection between previously failed intimate relationships as to behaviors and emotions that caused failure. (4, 8, 25)
26. Write a journal of sexual fantasies that stimulate sexual arousal. (18, 19, 26)
27. Implement new coital positions and settings for sexual activity that enhance pleasure and satisfaction. (27, 28)
28. Engage in more assertive behaviors that allow for sharing sexual needs, feelings, and desires; behaving more sensuously; and expressing pleasure. (26, 27, 28)
29. Resolve conflicts or develop coping strategies that reduce stress interfering with sexual interest or performance. (1, 2, 29)
30. Discuss low self-esteem issues that impede sexual functioning and verbalize positive self-image. (5, 6, 7, 30)
31. Communicate feelings of threat to partner that are based on perception of partner being too sexually aggressive. (28, 30, 31)

23. Assign books that provide accurate sexual information and/or outline sexual exercises that disinhibit and reinforce sexual sensate focus.
24. Explore sex role models client has experienced in childhood or adolescence.
25. Explore client's fears surrounding intimate relationships and whether there is evidence of repeated failure in this area.
26. Encourage development of an indulgence in sexual fantasies that mediate enhanced sexual desire.
27. Suggest experimentation with coital positions and settings for sexual play that may increase security, arousal, and satisfaction.
28. Encourage client to gradually explore role of being more sexually assertive, sensuously provocative, and freely uninhibited in sexual play with partner.
29. Probe stress in areas such as work, extended family, and social relationships that distract client from sexual desire or performance.
30. Explore fears of inadequacy as a sexual partner that led to sexual avoidance.
31. Explore feelings of threat brought on by perception of partner as sexually aggressive and demanding.

32. Openly acknowledge, if present, homosexual attraction. (8, 26, 32, 33)

33. Discuss feelings surrounding secret affair and make decision for termination of one of the relationships. (8, 33, 34)

34. Discuss feelings of and causes for depression. (1, 4, 29, 34, 35)

—. _____
_____

—. _____
_____

—. _____
_____

32. Explore homosexual interest that accounts for heterosexual disinterest.

33. Discuss any secret sexual affairs that may account for sexual dysfunction with partner.

34. Assess role of depression in suppressing sexual desire.

35. Refer for antidepressant medication prescription to alleviate depression.

—. _____
_____

—. _____
_____

—. _____
_____

DIAGNOSTIC SUGGESTIONS

Axis I:		
	302.71	Hypoactive Sexual Desire Disorder
	302.79	Sexual Aversion Disorder
	302.72	Female Sexual Arousal Disorder
	302.73	Female Orgasmic Disorder
	302.76	Dyspareunia
	306.51	Vaginismus
	V61.21	Sexual Abuse of Child (995.53, Victim)
	625.8	Female Hypoactive Sexual Desire Disorder Due to (Axis III Disorder)
	625.0	Female Dyspareunia Due to (Axis III Disorder)
	302.9	Sexual Disorder NOS
	_____	_____
	_____	_____

GRIEF/LOSS UNRESOLVED

BEHAVIORAL DEFINITIONS

1. Thoughts dominated by loss as client can focus on little else.
2. Serial losses in life (i.e., deaths, divorces, jobs) that led to depression and discouragement.
3. Strong emotional response exhibited when losses are discussed.
4. Symptoms of lack of appetite, weight loss, and/or insomnia as well as other depression signs that occurred since the loss.
5. Feelings of guilt that not enough was done for the lost significant other or unreasonable belief that client contributed to death of significant other.
6. Avoidance of talking on anything more than a superficial level about the loss.

—. _____

_____

—. _____

_____

—. _____

_____

LONG-TERM GOALS

1. Begin a healthy grieving process around the loss.
2. Develop awareness of how the avoidance of grieving has affected life and begin the healing process.
3. Complete the process of letting go of the lost significant other.
4. Resolve the loss and begin renewing old relationships and initiating new contacts with others.

—. _____

_____

_____

—. _____

_____

SHORT-TERM OBJECTIVES

1. Identify losses in life. (8, 18)
2. Increase understanding of the steps in the grief process. (1, 2, 10)
3. Identify where client is in the continuum of the grieving process. (1, 5, 6)
4. Begin verbalizing feelings associated with the loss. (3, 4, 5, 6, 7, 9)
5. State how the use of substances has aided the avoidance of feelings associated with the loss. (5, 19)
6. Tell the story of the loss. (8, 9, 12, 14)
7. Increase awareness of how avoiding dealing with the loss has negatively impacted client's life. (2, 9, 11, 19)
8. Identify the positive things about the deceased loved one and/or relationship and how these things may be remembered. (12, 13, 14, 17)

THERAPEUTIC INTERVENTIONS

1. Educate the client on the stages of the grieving process and answer any questions.
2. Ask client to read the books *Good Grief* (Westberg); *How Can It Be All Right When Everything Is All Wrong* (Smedes); *How to Survive the Loss of a Love* (Colgrove); *When Bad Things Happen to Good People* (Kushner); or another book on grief and loss; and process several key concepts with therapist.
3. Ask client to write a letter to lost person describing how he/she feels and read the letter to therapist.
4. Assign client to write about the loss with a special focus on the last contact with the person.
5. Assist client in identifying and expressing feelings connected with the loss in individual and/or group sessions.

The numbers in parentheses accompanying the short-term objectives correspond to the list of suggested therapeutic interventions.

9. Acknowledge dependency on lost loved one and begin to refocus life on independent actions to meet emotional needs. (4, 5, 11, 15, 17)

10. Verbalize and resolve feelings of anger or guilt focused on self or deceased loved one that blocks grief process. (15, 16, 17)

___. _____
_____

___. _____
_____

___. _____
_____

6. Assign client to keep a daily grief journal to be shared in therapy sessions.

7. Explore feelings of guilt and blame surrounding the loss.

8. Ask client to elaborate in an autobiography on the circumstances, feelings, and effects of the loss or losses in life and process with therapist.

9. Ask client to attend a grief/loss support group and report to therapist how he/she felt about attending.

10. Ask client to interview/talk to several people about losses in their lives regarding how they felt and coped. Process findings with therapist.

11. Assign client to write a good-bye letter to significant other and process letter with therapist.

12. Ask client to bring pictures or mementos connected with the loss to a session and talk about them with therapist.

13. Develop a grieving ritual with an identified feeling state on which client may focus near the anniversary of the loss. Process afterward with client what he/she received from the ritual.

14. Conduct a family and/or group session with the client participating where each member talks about his/her experience related to the loss.

15. Conduct an "empty chair" exercise with the client where he/she focuses on expressing to lost loved one imagined in the empty chair what he/she never said while that loved one was present.

16. Assign client to complete an exercise related to forgiveness and process it with therapist in an individual session.

17. Assign client to visit the grave of loved one and then process this experience and what it was like with therapist.

18. Assist client in identifying and sharing feelings about losses.

19. Ask client to list ways avoidance of grieving has negatively impacted his/her life.

___. _____

_____

___. _____

_____

___. _____

_____

DIAGNOSTIC SUGGESTIONS

Axis I:	296.2x	Major Depressive Disorder, Single Episode
	296.3x	Major Depressive Disorder, Recurrent
	V62.82	Bereavement
	309.0	Adjustment Disorder with Depressed Mood
	309.3	Adjustment Disorder with Disturbance of Conduct
	300.4	Dysthymic Disorder
	_____	_____
	_____	_____

IMPULSE CONTROL DISORDER

BEHAVIORAL DEFINITIONS

1. Several episodes of loss of control of aggressive impulses out of proportion to the situation and resulting in assaultive acts or destruction of property.
2. Deliberate fire-setting more than once for no personal gain and not to express direct anger or a fascination with fire.
3. Pattern of impulsively pulling out hair leading to significant hair loss.
4. Recurrent behavior of stealing objects not needed for personal use or monetary value.
5. A sense of tension or affective arousal before engaging in the impulsive behavior (e.g., kleptomania, pyromania, or trichotillomania).
6. A sense of pleasure, gratification, or release at the time of committing the ego-dystonic act.
7. A consistent pattern of acting before thinking that has resulted in numerous negative impacts on his/her life.
8. Excessive shifting from one activity to another and rarely, if ever, completing anything that is started.
9. Difficulty organizing things or self without supervision.
10. Difficulty waiting for things—that is, restless standing in line, talking out over others in a group, and the like.
11. Failure to resist an impulse, desire, or temptation to perform some act that is harmful to self or others.

—. _____
_____

—. _____
_____

—. _____
_____

LONG-TERM GOALS

1. Establish the ability to effectively channel impulses.
2. Decrease the frequency of impulsive acts.
3. Recognize and understand the emotional need met by the impulsive behavior while beginning to develop ways to block the impulses.

—. _____

_____

—. _____

_____

—. _____

_____

SHORT-TERM OBJECTIVES

1. Identify the symptoms of impulsivity. (1, 3, 9, 10)

2. Increase the ability to connect impulsivity with life difficulties. (6, 13)

3. Increase the ability for self-observation. (3, 10, 13)

4. Decrease the level of resistance to accepting feedback on behavior from significant others. (1, 7, 8)

5. Decrease the overall frequency of impulsive actions. (1, 2, 4)

6. Increase the time intervals between impulsive acts. (1, 2, 5)

THERAPEUTIC INTERVENTIONS

1. Monitor, encourage, redirect, and give feedback to client as necessary relating to control over impulsive actions.

2. Train client in impulse control techniques and assist in implementing them in daily life.

3. Assist client in increasing ability to observe self.

4. Assign client to read the book *What to Say When You Talk to Yourself* (Helmstetter) and process key ideas with therapist.

The numbers in parentheses accompanying the short-term objectives correspond to the list of suggested therapeutic interventions.

7. Develop and implement specific coping strategies to resist impulsive urges. (4, 5, 8)

8. Demonstrate verbally or in writing the ability to be reflective about his/her behavior (what, how,. etc.) (3, 6, 9)

9. Complete an evaluation for medication. (11)

10. Take medication as prescribed and report any side effects to therapist and/or physician. (12)

11. Verbalize an understanding of the tension, anxiety, and feelings of helplessness that precede the impulsive acts. (3, 9, 10)

12. Verbalize the causes for the anxiety or frustration that accompany the impulsive behavior. (9, 10)

—. _____

_____

—. _____

_____

—. _____

_____

5. Assist client and significant others in developing and putting into effect a reward system for deterring impulsive actions.

6. Ask client to make a list of positive things he/she gets from impulsive actions and process it with therapist.

7. Conduct a session with spouse, parents, or significant others to increase communication skills and behavior expectations with client.

8. Conduct a session with spouse/significant other and client to develop a bargaining contract for receiving feedback prior to or following impulsive acts.

9. Assist client in developing ability to analyze his/her behavior and the feelings associated with the impulsive behavior.

10. Ask client to keep a log of impulsive acts (time, place, thoughts, what was going on prior to act) and process log with therapist.

11. Refer and arrange for client to have a physician evaluation for medications.

12. Monitor client for compliance, side effects, and overall effectiveness of the medication. Redirect client when necessary and consult with prescribing physician at regular intervals.

13. Assist client in making connections between his/her impulsivity and negative consequences experienced.

—. _____

_____

—. _____

_____

—. _____

_____

DIAGNOSTIC SUGGESTIONS

Axis I: 312.34   Intermittent Explosive Disorder
312.32   Kleptomania
312.31   Pathological Gambling
312.39   Trichotillomania
312.30   Impulse Control Disorder NOS
312.33   Pyromania
310.1   Personality Change Due to (Axis III Disorder)

_____   _____

_____   _____

Axis II: 301.7   Antisocial Personality Disorder
301.83   Borderline Personality Disorder

_____   _____

_____   _____

INTIMATE RELATIONSHIP CONFLICTS

BEHAVIORAL DEFINITIONS

1. Frequent or continual arguing with spouse or significant other.
2. Lack of communication with spouse or significant other.
3. A pattern of angry projection of responsibility for the conflicts on the other party.
4. Marital separation(s).
5. Pending divorce.
6. Involvement in multiple intimate relationships at the same time.
7. Physical and/or verbal abuse in a relationship.
8. A pattern of superficial or no communication, infrequent or no sexual contact, excessive involvement in activities (work or recreation) that allows for avoidance of closeness to spouse.
9. A pattern of repeated broken, conflictual relationships due to personal deficiencies in maintaining a trust relationship or choosing abusive or dysfunctional partners.

—. _____
   _____
—. _____
   _____
—. _____
   _____

LONG-TERM GOALS

1. Accept the termination of the relationship.
2. Increase awareness of client's role in the relationship conflicts.
3. Develop the ability to handle conflicts in a mature, controlled, nonaggressive, and/or assertive way.
4. Develop mutual respect for significant other in the relationship.
5. Learn to identify escalating behaviors that lead to abuse.
6. Make a decision in terms of commitment to one intimate relationship at a time.
7. Develop the necessary skills for effective, open, mutually satisfying communication, sexual intimacy, and enjoyable time for companionship within the relationship.

—. _____

_____

—. _____

_____

—. _____

_____

SHORT-TERM OBJECTIVES

1. Identify the causes for past and present conflicts within the relationship. (9, 10, 11, 12, 15)

2. Identify his/her role in the conflicts. (3, 5, 18, 19)

3. Identify ways to initiate personal change to improve the relationship. (2, 7, 10, 14)

4. Increase the frequency and quality of the communication with spouse/significant other. (1, 6, 13)

THERAPEUTIC INTERVENTIONS

1. Assign client to talk daily with spouse about prechosen, nonemotional topics for 5 minutes without arguing. Increase time and degree of depth with success.

2. Assign client to read the book *The Intimate Enemy* (Bach and Wyden) and process key ideas with therapist.

The numbers in parentheses accompanying the short-term objectives correspond to the list of suggested therapeutic interventions.

5. Decrease the intensity and frequency of conflictual interactions in the relationship. (1, 2, 3, 7)

6. Identify and verbalize needs both partners have in the relationship. (6, 7, 13, 14)

7. Verbally recognize client's responsibility to meet some needs of significant other in the relationship. (7, 10, 11, 12)

8. Develop and verbalize an understanding of the connection between substance abuse and the conflicts present within the relationship. (3, 5, 10, 14)

9. Identify the positive and negative aspects of client's present relationship. (7, 8, 10, 11, 14)

10. Increase awareness of patterns in repeatedly forming destructive intimate relationships. (15, 18, 19)

11. Identify and express feelings regarding the relationship conflicts. (2, 4, 6, 9)

12. Discuss the level of closeness/distance desired in a relationship and how this may relate to fears of intimacy. (7, 13, 18, 19)

13. Arrange, attend, and actively participate in conjoint sessions with spouse or significant other. (6, 13, 14, 20)

14. Identify changes the significant other should make to improve the quality of the relationship. (11, 14)

3. Ask client to make a list of escalating behaviors that occur prior to abusive behavior.

4. Refer to assertiveness-training classes.

5. Confront avoidance of responsibility for conflicts within the relationship.

6. Facilitate conjoint sessions with significant other with focus on increasing communication skills.

7. Assist client in identifying behaviors that focus on relationship building.

8. Ask client to make a list of positive things about the relationship and positive things about significant other.

9. Process current, ongoing conflicts regarding the relationship.

10. Assign and process a list of changes client needs to make to improve relationship.

11. Assign and process a list of changes client's significant other needs to make to improve relationship.

12. Ask significant other to make list of changes needed for self and other to improve relationship.

13. Hold conjoint sessions to clarify communication and expression of feelings of each partner for the other.

15. Verbalize the various feelings associated with grieving the loss of the relationship (e.g., denial, guilt, anger, embarrassment, fear, loneliness). (16)

16. Develop a plan for meeting social and emotional needs during separation and divorce. (17)

17. Rebuild positive self-image after acceptance of the rejection associated with the broken relationship. (4, 17)

18. Increase time spent in enjoyable contact with spouse. (1, 7, 20)

19. Increase frequency and quality of sexual contact with spouse. (8, 9, 20, 21)

20. Initiate verbal and physical affection behaviors toward spouse. (7, 13, 20, 21)

__. _____
   _____

__. _____
   _____

__. _____
   _____

14. In conjoint sessions, process changes each partner believes are necessary to improve the relationship.

15. Probe family of origin history of each partner to see patterns of intimate relationship interaction repeating themselves in the present relationship.

16. Explore and clarify feelings associated with loss of the relationship.

17. Encourage and support building new social relationships to overcome withdrawal and fear of failure.

18. Explore needs that motivate maintaining multiple intimate relationships.

19. Discuss the consequences to self and others that result from multiple intimate relationships.

20. Assist in planning rewarding, shared social/recreational activities with spouse.

21. Diffuse resistance surrounding initiating affectionate or sexual interactions with spouse.

__. _____
   _____

__. _____
   _____

__. _____
   _____

DIAGNOSTIC SUGGESTIONS

Axis I:	312.34	Intermittent Explosive Disorder
	309.0	Adjustment Disorder with Depressed Mood
	309.24	Adjustment Disorder with Anxiety
	300.4	Dysthymic Disorder
	300.00	Anxiety Disorder NOS
	311	Depressive Disorder NOS
	309.81	Posttraumatic Stress Disorder
	_____	_____
	_____	_____
Axis II:	301.20	Schizoid Personality Disorder
	301.81	Narcissistic Personality Disorder
	301.9	Personality Disorder NOS
	_____	_____
	_____	_____

LEGAL CONFLICTS

BEHAVIORAL DEFINITIONS

1. Legal charges pending.
2. Parole or probation subsequent to conviction on legal charges.
3. Legal pressure that has been central to the decision to enter treatment.
4. A long history of criminal activity leading to numerous incarcerations.
5. Chemical dependence resulting in several arrests and current court involvement.

—. _____

_____

—. _____

_____

—. _____

_____

LONG-TERM GOALS

1. Accept and responsibly respond to the mandates of court.
2. Understand how chemical dependence has contributed to legal problems and accept the need for recovery.
3. Accept responsibility for decisions and actions that have led to arrests and develop higher moral and ethical standards to govern behavior.
4. Internalize the need for treatment so as to change values, thoughts, feelings, and behavior to a more pro-social position.

—. _____

    _____

    _____

—. _____

    _____

    _____

—. _____

    _____

SHORT-TERM OBJECTIVES

1. Make regular contact with court officers to fulfill sentencing requirements. (1)
2. Verbalize the role drug and/or alcohol abuse has played in legal problems. (2, 3)
3. State a desire to remain abstinent. (4, 5)
4. Maintain sobriety in accordance with rules of probation/parole. (4, 5)
5. Verbalize and accept responsibility for series of decisions and actions that eventually led to illegal activity. (6, 7, 8)
6. State values that affirm behavior within the boundaries of the law. (7, 8)
7. Verbalize how emotional state of anger, frustration, helplessness, or depression has contributed to illegal behavior. (9, 10, 11)

THERAPEUTIC INTERVENTIONS

1. Monitor and encourage client to keep appointments with court officers.
2. Explore issue of chemical dependence and how it may have contributed to legal conflicts.
3. Confront denial of chemical dependence by reviewing various negative consequences of addiction.
4. Reinforce need for a plan for recovery and sobriety as means of improving judgment and control over behavior.
5. Monitor and reinforce sobriety, using physiological measures to confirm, if advisable.
6. Assist client in clarification of values that allow illegal actions.
7. Discuss values associated with respecting legal

The numbers in parentheses accompanying the short-term objectives correspond to the list of suggested therapeutic interventions.

8. Identify the causes for negative emotional state that was associated with illegal actions. (9, 10, 11, 12)

9. Discuss alternative coping mechanisms for negative emotions that reduce the potential for breaking the law. (12, 13, 14)

__. _____

_____

__. _____

_____

__. _____

_____

boundaries and the rights of others as well as the consequences of crossing these boundaries.

8. Confront denial and projection of responsibility onto others for own illegal actions.

9. Probe negative emotional states that could contribute to illegal behavior.

10. Explore causes for underlying negative emotions that consciously or unconsciously foster criminal behavior.

11. Refer client for ongoing counseling to deal with emotional conflicts and antisocial impulses.

12. Interpret antisocial behavior that is linked to current or past emotional conflicts to foster insight and resolution.

13. Assess and clarify cognitive belief structures that foster illegal behavior.

14. Restructure cognition to foster keeping of legal boundaries and respecting the rights of others.

__. _____

_____

__. _____

_____

__. _____

_____

DIAGNOSTIC SUGGESTIONS

Axis I:	304.20	Cocaine Dependence
	303.90	Alcohol Dependence
	312.32	Kleptomania
	V71.01	Adult Antisocial Behavior
	309.3	Adjustment Disorder with Disturbance of Conduct
	_____	_____
	_____	_____
Axis II:	301.7	Antisocial Personality Disorder
	_____	_____
	_____	_____

LOW SELF-ESTEEM

BEHAVIORAL DEFINITIONS

1. Inability to accept compliments.
2. Self-disparaging remarks; takes blame easily.
3. Lack of pride in grooming.
4. Difficulty in saying no to others; assumes not being liked by others.
5. Fear of rejection of others, especially peer group.
6. Lack of any goals for life and setting of inappropriately low goals for self.
7. Verbalization of dislike for self (sees self as unattractive, worthless, a burden, unimportant).
8. Inability to identify positive things about self.

—. _____
   _____
   _____
—. _____
   _____
   _____
—. _____
   _____

LONG-TERM GOALS

1. Elevate self-esteem.
2. Develop a consistent, positive self image.
3. Demonstrate improved self-esteem through more pride in appearance, more assertiveness, greater eye contact, and identification of positive traits in self-talk messages.

—. _____
   _____

___. _____

     _____

     _____

___. _____

     _____

SHORT-TERM OBJECTIVES

1. Increase awareness of self-disparaging statements. (1, 2, 5, 17)

2. Decrease frequency of negative self-statements. (1, 3, 15, 17)

3. Increase frequency of assertive behaviors. (5, 6, 11)

4. Decrease fear of rejection while increasing sense of self-acceptance. (5, 7, 11, 15)

5. Identify positive things about self. (3, 4, 11, 16)

6. Increase eye contact with others. (3, 8, 9)

7. Identify verbally and/or in writing needs for self and a plan for assertively satisfying those needs. (6, 17)

8. Identify accomplishments that can be done to improve self-image and a plan to achieve those goals. (10, 5)

9. Increase insight into the historical and current sources of low self-esteem. (5, 7, 13, 15)

THERAPEUTIC INTERVENTIONS

1. Confront and reframe client's self-disparaging comments.

2. Reinforce client's positive self-descriptive statements.

3. Assign mirror exercises of client talking positively about self.

4. Assign client to make one positive self-statement daily and record it in a journal.

5. Assist client in processing self-esteem issues in group and individual therapy.

6. Train in assertiveness or refer client to a group that will educate and facilitate assertiveness skills via lectures and assignments.

7. Help client become aware of fear of rejection and its connection with past rejection or abandonment experiences.

8. Confront client when he/she is observed avoiding eye contact with others.

The numbers in parentheses accompanying the short-term objectives correspond to the list of suggested therapeutic interventions.

10. Take responsibility for daily grooming and personal hygiene. (5, 12)

11. Positively acknowledge verbal compliments from others. (5, 6, 9)

12. Form realistic, appropriate, and attainable goals for self in all areas of life. (10, 15)

13. Take verbal responsibility for accomplishments without discounting. (6, 11)

14. Identify negative self-talk messages used to reinforce low self-esteem. (1, 5, 14, 15, 17)

15. Use positive self-talk messages to build self-esteem. (11, 14, 16, 17)

—. _____

_____

—. _____

_____

—. _____

_____

9. Assign client to make eye contact with whomever he/she is speaking to.

10. Help client analyze goals to make sure they are realistic and attainable.

11. Reinforce verbally the use of positive statements of confidence and accomplishments.

12. Monitor and give feedback when necessary to client on his/her grooming and hygiene.

13. Discuss, emphasize, and interpret incidents of abuse (emotional, physical, and sexual) and how they have impacted feelings about self.

14. Assign client to read *What to Say When You Talk to Yourself* (Helmstetter) and process key ideas with therapist.

15. Help client identify distorted, negative beliefs about self and the world.

16. Reinforce use of more realistic, positive messages to self in interpreting life events.

17. Ask client to complete and process an exercise in the book *Ten Days to Self Esteem!* (Burns).

—. _____

_____

—. _____

_____

—. _____

_____

DIAGNOSTIC SUGGESTIONS

Axis I: 300.23   Social Phobia
300.4   Dysthymic Disorder
296.xx   Major Depressive Disorder
296.xx   Bipolar I Disorder
296.89   Bipolar II Disorder

_____   _____

_____   _____

MALE SEXUAL DYSFUNCTION

BEHAVIORAL DEFINITIONS

1. Consistently very low or no pleasurable anticipation of or desire for sexual activity.
2. Strong avoidance of and/or repulsion to any and all sexual contact in spite of a relationship of mutual caring and respect.
3. Recurrent lack of usual physiological response of sexual excitement and arousal (attaining and/or maintaining an erection).
4. Consistent lack of subjective sense of enjoyment and pleasure during sexual activity.
5. Persistent delay in or absence of reaching orgasm (ejaculation) after achieving arousal and in spite of sensitive sexual pleasuring by a caring partner.
6. Genital pain before, during, or after sexual intercourse.

—. _____
   _____
—. _____
   _____
—. _____
   _____

LONG-TERM GOALS

1. Increase desire for and enjoyment of sexual activity.
2. Attain and maintain physiological excitement response during sexual intercourse.
3. Reach orgasm (ejaculation) with a reasonable amount of time, intensity, and focus to sexual stimulation.

4. Eliminate pain and achieve a presence of subjective pleasure before, during, and after sexual intercourse.

—. _____

_____

—. _____

_____

—. _____

_____

SHORT-TERM OBJECTIVES

1. Share thoughts and feelings regarding relationship with sexual partner. (1, 2)

2. Openly discuss with partner conflicts and unfulfilled needs in the relationship that lead to anger and emotional distance. (1, 2)

3. Discuss sexual attitudes learned in family of origin experiences. (3, 8, 9, 10)

4. Verbalize positive and healthy sexual attitudes. (11, 12, 18, 19, 23)

5. Describe negative feelings regarding sexual experiences of childhood or adolescence. (3, 4, 5, 9, 10)

6. Verbalize a resolution of feelings regarding sexual trauma or abuse experiences. (4, 5)

THERAPEUTIC INTERVENTIONS

1. Assess the relationship with sexual partner as to level of harmony and fulfillment.

2. Direct conjoint sessions that focus on conflict resolution, expression of feelings, and sex education.

3. Probe family of origin history for causes of inhibition, guilt, fear, or repulsion.

4. Probe client's history for experience of sexual trauma or abuse.

5. Process emotions surrounding an emotional trauma in the sexual arena.

6. Assess role of depression in suppressing sexual desire or performance.

7. Refer for antidepressant medication prescription to alleviate depression.

The numbers in parentheses accompanying the short-term objectives correspond to the list of suggested therapeutic interventions.

7. Discuss feelings of and causes for depression. (1, 4, 6, 7, 29)

8. State acceptance of sexual feelings and behavior as normal and healthy. (13, 14, 18, 19, 23)

9. Provide a detailed sexual history that explores all experiences that influence sexual attitudes, feelings, and behavior. (3, 8, 9, 10)

10. Verbalize an understanding of role of family of origin experiences in development of negative sexual attitudes and responses. (3, 8, 9, 10)

11. State an understanding of how religious training negatively influenced sexual thoughts, feelings, and behavior. (8, 9, 10, 11)

12. Verbalize negative cognitive messages that trigger fears, shame, anger, or grief during sex activity. (11, 19, 30)

13. Verbalize the development of positive and healthy automatic thoughts that mediate relaxed pleasure. (12, 13, 14, 18)

14. Practice sensate focus exercises alone and with partner and share feelings associated with activity. (14, 19, 20, 27)

15. Abstain from substance abuse patterns that interfere with sexual response. (8, 15)

8. Obtain a detailed sexual history that examines current adult sexual functioning as well as childhood and adolescent experiences, level and sources of sexual knowledge, typical sexual practices and frequency of them, medical history, and use of mood-altering substances.

9. Explore role of family of origin in teaching negative attitudes regarding sexuality.

10. Explore role of religious training in reinforcing feelings of guilt and shame surrounding sexual behavior and thoughts.

11. Probe automatic thoughts that trigger negative emotions before, during, and after sexual activity.

12. Train client in healthy alternative thoughts that will mediate pleasure, relaxation, and disinhibition.

13. Give permission for less inhibited, less constricted sexual behavior by assigning body-pleasuring exercises with partner.

14. Assign body exploration and awareness exercises that reduce inhibition and desensitize client to sexual aversion.

15. Assess the possible role that substance abuse, diabetes, hypertension, or thyroid disease may have on sexual functioning.

16. Verbalize an understanding of the role physical disease or medication has on sexual dysfunction. (16, 17)

17. Cooperate with a physician's complete examination and report results. (17)

18. Demonstrate healthy and accurate knowledge of sexuality by freely verbalizing adequate information of sexual functioning using appropriate terms for sexually related body parts. (18, 19, 23)

19. Write about sexual feelings and thoughts in a daily journal. (18, 19, 26)

20. Verbalize increasing desire for and pleasure with sexual activity. (18, 19, 20, 27, 28)

21. Discuss feelings surrounding secret affair and make termination decision on one of the relationships. (6, 21, 30)

22. Openly acknowledge and discuss, if present, homosexual attraction. (11, 19, 21, 22)

23. Read and discuss books assigned on human sexuality. (23)

24. Verbalize an understanding of the connection between lack of positive sex role model in childhood and current adult sexual dysfunction. (3, 8, 9, 24)

16. Review medications taken by client with regard to their possible negative side effects on sexual functioning.

17. Refer to a physician for a complete physical to rule out any organic basis for dysfunction.

18. Disinhibit and educate the client by talking freely and respectfully regarding sexual body parts, sexual feelings, and sexual behavior.

19. Assign client to keep a journal of sexual thoughts and feelings to increase awareness and acceptance of them as normal.

20. Assign graduated steps of sexual pleasuring exercises with partner that reduce performance anxiety and focus on experiencing bodily arousal sensations.

21. Discuss any secret sexual affairs that may account for sexual dysfunction with partner.

22. Explore homosexual interest that accounts for heterosexual disinterest.

23. Assign books that provide accurate sexual information and/or outline sexual exercises that disinhibit and reinforce sexual sensate focus.

24. Explore sex role models client has experienced in childhood or adolescence.

25. Verbalize connection between previously failed
intimate relationships as to
behaviors and emotions
that caused failure.
(8, 25, 30, 31)

26. Write a journal of sexual
fantasies that stimulate
sexual arousal. (19, 26)

27. Implement new coital
positions and settings for
sexual activity that enhance
pleasure and satisfaction.
(23, 27, 28)

28. Engage in more assertive
behaviors that allow for
sharing sexual needs,
feelings, and desires; behaving more sensuously and
expressing pleasure.
(13, 26, 27, 28)

29. Resolve conflicts or develop
coping strategies that
reduce stress interfering
with sexual interest or
performance. (6, 29, 30)

30. Discuss low self-esteem
issues that impede sexual
functioning and verbalize
positive self-image.
(4, 9, 10, 30)

31. Communicate feelings of
threat to partner that are
based on perception of
partner being too sexually
aggressive. (2, 30, 31)

32. Implement the squeeze
technique during sexual
intercourse and report on
success and feelings. (32)

25. Explore client's fears surrounding intimate relationships and whether there is
evidence of repeated failure
in this area.

26. Encourage development of
an indulgence in sexual
fantasies that mediate
enhanced sexual desire.

27. Suggest experimentation
with coital positions and
settings for sexual play that
may increase security,
arousal, and satisfaction.

28. Encourage client to gradually explore role of being
more sexually assertive,
sensuously provocative, and
freely uninhibited in sexual
play with partner.

29. Probe stress in areas such
as work, extended family,
and social relationships
that distract client from
sexual desire or perfor-
mance.

30. Explore fears of inadequacy
as a sexual partner that led
to sexual avoidance.

31. Explore feelings of threat
brought on by perception of
partner as sexually aggressive.

32. Instruct client and partner
in use of squeeze technique
to retard premature ejaculation.

___. _____   ___. _____

      _____   _____

___. _____   ___. _____

      _____   _____

___. _____   ___. _____

      _____   _____

DIAGNOSTIC SUGGESTIONS

Axis I:	302.71	Hypoactive Sexual Desire Disorder
	302.79	Sexual Aversion Disorder
	302.72	Male Erectile Disorder
	302.74	Male Orgasmic Disorder
	302.76	Dyspareunia
	302.75	Premature Ejaculation
	608.89	Male Hypoactive Sexual Disorder Due to (Axis III Disorder)
	607.84	Male Erectile Disorder Due to (Axis III Disorder)
	608.89	Male Dyspareunia Due to (Axis III Disorder)
	302.9	Sexual Disorder NOS
	V61.21	Sexual Abuse of Child (995.5, Victim)
	_____	_____
	_____	_____

MANIA OR HYPOMANIA

BEHAVIORAL DEFINITIONS

1. Loquaciousness or pressured speech.
2. Flight of ideas or reports of thoughts racing.
3. Grandiosity and/or persecutory beliefs.
4. Decreased need for sleep often with little or no appetite.
5. Increased motor activity or agitation.
6. Poor attention span and easily distracted.
7. Loss of normal inhibition leading to impulsive, pleasure-oriented behavior without regard for painful consequences.
8. Bizarre dress and grooming.
9. Expansive mood that can easily turn to impatience and irritable anger if behavior is blocked or confronted.
10. Lack of follow-through in projects even though energy is very high since behavior lacks discipline and goal-directedness.

—. _____
   _____
—. _____
   _____
—. _____
   _____

LONG-TERM GOALS

1. Reduce psychic energy and return to normal activity levels, good judgment, stable mood, and goal-directed behavior.
2. Reduce agitation, impulsivity, and pressured speech while achieving sensitivity to the consequences of behavior and having more realistic expectations.

3. Talk about underlying feelings of low self-esteem or guilt and fears of rejection, dependency, and abandonment.
4. Achieve controlled behavior, moderated mood, and more deliberative speech and thought process through psychotherapy and medication.

—. _____
_____
—. _____
_____
—. _____
_____

SHORT-TERM OBJECTIVES

1. Sleep about 5 hours or more per night. (1, 3, 6, 19)
2. Be less agitated and distracted—that is, able to sit quietly and calmly for 30 minutes. (2, 6, 10, 15, 18)
3. Decrease impulsivity in action—that is, not engaging in self-destructive behaviors such as over-spending, promiscuity, substance abuse, or use of profane language. (3, 6, 13, 15, 18)
4. Identify fears associated with rejection, failure, and abandonment. (7, 8, 9, 12)
5. Acknowledge and explore causes for low self-esteem that is covered by grandiosity. (9, 12, 14, 16)

THERAPEUTIC INTERVENTIONS

1. Assess stage of elation: hypomanic, manic, or psychotic.
2. Arrange for psychiatric evaluation for pharmacotherapy (e.g., lithium carbonate).
3. Arrange for or continue hospitalization if client is judged to be potentially harmful to self or others, or unable to care for own basic needs.
4. Meet with family to educate them regarding the illness and treatment.
5. Meet with family to allow ventilation of their feelings of guilt, shame, fear, confu-

_____

The numbers in parentheses accompanying the short-term objectives correspond to the list of suggested therapeutic interventions.

6. Speak more slowly and be more subject-focused. (2, 6, 10, 11)

7. Achieve mood stability—that is, slower to react with anger and less expansive or elevated. (2, 11, 13, 19)

8. Pay attention to dressing and grooming appropriately, not in an attention-getting manner. (1, 5, 15, 17)

9. Take psychotropic medications as directed. (2, 4, 19)

—. _____
   _____

—. _____
   _____

—. _____
   _____

sion, or anger regarding client's behavior.

6. Provide structure and focus to client's thoughts and action by establishing plans and routine.

7. Reassure client regarding therapist's ability to be trusted not to reject or abandon him/her.

8. Confront denial of dependency needs and fear of intimacy.

9. Probe causes for low self-esteem and abandonment fears in family of origin history.

10. Facilitate impulse control by using role-play, behavioral rehearsal, and role reversal to increase sensitivity to consequences of behavior.

11. Verbally reinforce slower speech and more deliberate thought process.

12. Encourage client to share feelings at a deeper level to facilitate openness and intimacy in relationships, counteracting denial and superficiality.

13. Calmly listen to expressions of hostility while setting limits on aggressive or impulsive behavior.

14. Interpret fear and insecurity underlying braggadocio, hostility, and denial of dependency.

15. Assist client in setting reasonable goals and limits on behavior.

16. Assist client in identifying strengths and assets to build self-esteem and confidence.

17. Encourage and reinforce appropriate dress and grooming.

18. Set limits on manipulation or acting out by making clear rules and establishing clear consequences for breaking rules.

19. Monitor client for medication compliance and effectiveness.

—. _____
    _____

—. _____
    _____

—. _____
    _____

DIAGNOSTIC SUGGESTIONS

Axis I:	296.xx	Bipolar I Disorder
	296.89	Bipolar II Disorder
	301.13	Cyclothymic Disorder
	295.70	Schizoaffective Disorder
	296.80	Bipolar Disorder NOS
	310.1	Personality Change Due to (Axis III Disorder)
	_____	_____
	_____	_____

MEDICAL ISSUES

BEHAVIORAL DEFINITIONS

1. A diagnosed serious medical condition that needs attention and has an impact on daily living (e.g., high blood pressure, asthma, seizures, diabetes, heart disease, cancer, or cirrhosis).
2. Lack of prenatal care for a pregnant client.
3. A medical condition for which the client is under a physician's care.
4. A positive test for HIV (human immunodeficiency virus).
5. AIDS (acquired immune deficiency syndrome).
6. Constant pain, frequent headaches, constant tiredness, feeling generally unwell.
7. Medical complications secondary to chemical dependence.
8. Psychological or behavioral factors that influence the course of the medical condition.

LONG-TERM GOALS

1. Give birth to a healthy, chemically free infant.
2. Medically stabilize physical condition.
3. Alleviate acute medical condition.
4. Accept chronic or acute medical condition with proper medical attention given to it.

5. Resolve physical symptoms.
6. Stabilize medical condition and begin addiction recovery.
7. Accept the role of psychological or behavioral factors in development of medical condition and focus on resolution of these factors.

—. _____

_____

—. _____

_____

—. _____

_____

SHORT-TERM OBJECTIVES

1. Comply totally with doctor's orders for tests, medications, limitations, and/or treatments. (1, 4)

2. Increase knowledge of medical condition. (2, 5, 8, 9)

3. Demonstrate responsibility by taking prescribed medication(s) consistently and on time. (1, 7)

4. Develop steps for follow-up medical care for medical condition. (6, 9)

5. Report any symptoms experienced or side effects from medication to physicians or therapists. (1)

6. Identify how chemical dependency has negatively impacted medical condition. (3, 5, 9)

THERAPEUTIC INTERVENTIONS

1. Monitor and document client's follow-through on doctor's orders and redirect when client is failing to comply.

2. Arrange for consultation with dietitian and other pertinent professionals.

3. Refer client to physician for complete physical.

4. Make any necessary arrangements required for client to obtain the medical services needed.

5. Work with client in group and individual sessions to increase understanding of how lifestyle negatively impacts medical condition.

_____

The numbers in parentheses accompanying the short-term objectives correspond to the list of suggested therapeutic interventions.

7. Identify emotional effects of medical condition. (7, 9)

8. Show verbal recognition of how emotional status can affect medical condition. (7, 9)

9. Decrease level of verbal denial regarding medical condition while increasing level of verbal acceptance. (1, 7, 9)

10. Increase knowledge of how proper nutrition can have a positive impact on medical condition. (2, 3, 7)

11. Identify how emotions and behavior have negatively impacted client's health. (5, 7)

12. Verbalize emotional, cognitive, and behavioral changes needed to improve health. (7, 10)

—. _____

_____

—. _____

_____

—. _____

_____

6. Process with client the necessary steps needed in order to ensure that proper medical attention is obtained.

7. Help client identify and express his/her feelings connected with medical condition.

8. Consult with physician and review doctor's orders with client.

9. Assign client to attend a support group related to his/her physical condition and report the positive aspects of attending to therapist.

10. Reinforce emotional stability, behavioral responsibility, and positive self-talk that reduces risk to health.

—. _____

_____

—. _____

_____

—. _____

_____

DIAGNOSTIC SUGGESTIONS

Axis I:	304.20	Cocaine Dependence
	303.90	Alcohol Dependence
	307.89	Pain Disorder Associated with Psychological Factors and (Axis III Disorder)
	307.80	Pain Disorder Associated with Psychological Factors
	300.7	Hypochondriasis
	300.81	Somatization Disorder
	316	Personality Traits Affecting (Axis III Disorder)
	316	Maladaptive Health Behaviors Affecting (Axis III Disorder)
	316	Psychological Symptoms Affecting (Axis III Disorder)

_____ _____

_____ _____

OBSESSIVE-COMPULSIVE BEHAVIORS

BEHAVIORAL DEFINITIONS

1. Recurrent and persistent ideas, thoughts, or impulses that are viewed as intrusive, senseless, and time-consuming, or that interfere with client's daily routine, job performance, or social relationships.
2. Failed attempts to ignore or control these thoughts or impulses or neutralize them with other thoughts and actions.
3. Recognition that obsessive thoughts are a product of his/her own mind.
4. Repetitive and intentional behaviors that are done in response to obsessive thoughts or according to eccentric rules.
5. Repetitive and excessive behavior that is done to neutralize or prevent discomfort or some dreaded situation; however, the behavior is not connected in any realistic way with what it is designed to neutralize or prevent.
6. Recognition of repetitive behaviors as excessive and unreasonable.

—. _____
_____

—. _____
_____

—. _____
_____

LONG-TERM GOALS

1. Reduce time involved with or interference from obsessions and compulsions.

2. Resolve key life conflicts and the emotional stress that fuels obsessive-compulsive behavior patterns.
3. Develop the ability to function daily at a consistent level with minimal interference from obsessions and compulsions.

___. _____

_____

___. _____

_____

___. _____

_____

SHORT-TERM OBJECTIVES

1. Take medication as prescribed and report any improvement or side effects to therapist. (1, 2)
2. Decrease frequency of obsessive-compulsive behaviors that interfere with daily functioning. (3, 4, 7, 8)
3. Implement thought-stopping technique to interrupt obsessions. (3)
4. Practice relaxation methods to reduce tension. (4)
5. Utilize biofeedback to improve relaxation ability. (4, 5)
6. Identify key life conflicts that raise anxiety. (6, 7)
7. Verbalize and clarify feelings connected to key life conflicts. (6, 7)

THERAPEUTIC INTERVENTIONS

1. Arrange for a medication evaluation for client to be placed on serotonin blocker (e.g., Anafranil, Prozac, Effexor) if appropriate.
2. Monitor and evaluate client's medication compliance and the effectiveness of the medications on level of functioning.
3. Assign thought-stopping technique that cognitively interferes with obsessions by thinking of a stop sign and then a pleasant scene.
4. Train in relaxation methods to counteract high anxiety.
5. Administer biofeedback to deepen client's relaxation skill.

The numbers in parentheses accompanying the short-term objectives correspond to the list of suggested therapeutic interventions.

8. Decrease level of intensity around conflicts. (3, 4, 5, 6)

9. Verbally accept and implement the intervention tasks as assigned by therapist. (9, 10, 11, 12)

10. Develop and implement a daily ritual that interrupts the current pattern of compulsions. (10, 12)

11. Verbally accept and integrate the therapist's reframing into client's thinking/behavior. (11)

—. _____
_____

—. _____
_____

—. _____
_____

6. Encourage, support, and assist client in identifying and expressing feelings related to key unresolved life issues.

7. Explore with client his/her life circumstances to help identify key unresolved conflicts.

8. Assist client in developing self-talk as a strategy to help abate his/her obsessive thoughts.

9. Develop and assign a cognitive/behavioral intervention task that will help disrupt the obsessive-compulsive patterns.

10. Develop and assign an Ericksonian task to the client that is centered around the obsession or compulsion and assess the results with client.

11. Create and sell to client a reframing of his/her obsessions and/or compulsion. Monitor the results in follow-up sessions with client.

12. Help client create and implement a ritual. Follow up with client on the outcome of its implementation and make any necessary adjustments.

___. _____

_____

___. _____

_____

___. _____

_____

DIAGNOSTIC SUGGESTIONS

Axis I: 300.3   Obsessive-Compulsive Disorder
           300.00   Anxiety Disorder NOS
           296.xx   Major Depressive Disorder
           303.90   Alcohol Dependence
           304.10   Sedative, Hypnotic, or Anxiolytic Dependence

           _____   _____

           _____   _____

Axis II: 301.82   Avoidant Personality Disorder
           301.4   Obsessive-Compulsive Personality Disorder

           _____   _____

           _____   _____

PARANOID IDEATION

BEHAVIORAL DEFINITIONS

1. Extreme or consistent distrust of others generally or someone specifically, without sufficient basis.
2. Expectation of being exploited or harmed by others.
3. Misinterpretation of benign events as having threatening personal significance.
4. Hypersensitivity to hints of personal critical judgment by others.
5. Inclination to keep distance from others out of fear of being hurt or taken advantage of.
6. Tendency to be easily offended and quick to anger; defensive behavior.
7. A pattern of being suspicious of loyalty or fidelity of spouse or significant other, without reason.

LONG-TERM GOALS

1. Show more trust in others by speaking positively of them and reporting comfort in socializing.
2. Interact with others without defensiveness or anger.
3. Verbalize trust of significant other and eliminate accusations of disloyalty.

4. Report reduced vigilance and suspicion around others as well as more relaxed, trusting, and open interaction.

—. _____

_____

—. _____

_____

—. _____

_____

SHORT-TERM OBJECTIVES

1. Identify core belief that others are untrustworthy and malicious. (1, 2, 11, 12)

2. Make verbal connection between fears of others and own feelings of inadequacy. (3, 4, 5)

3. Agree to collaborate with the therapist in probing feelings of vulnerability. (3, 4, 5)

4. Identify historical sources of feelings of vulnerability. (5, 6)

5. Acknowledge that belief about others being threatening is based on more subjective interpretation than on objective data. (2, 7, 8, 9)

6. Verbalize trust of significant other and feel relaxed when not in his/her presence. (2, 6, 9, 10)

THERAPEUTIC INTERVENTIONS

1. Assist client in seeing the pattern of distrusting others.

2. Provide alternative explanations for others' behavior that counter client's pattern of assumption of others' malicious intent.

3. Probe client's fears of personal inadequacy and vulnerability.

4. Interpret client's fears of own anger as basis for mistrust of others.

5. Explore historical sources of feelings of vulnerability in family of origin experiences.

6. Review social interactions of client and explore distorted cognitive beliefs operative during interactions.

The numbers in parentheses accompanying the short-term objectives correspond to the list of suggested therapeutic interventions.

7. Not be accusatory of others. (7, 9)

8. Interact socially without fear or suspicion being reported. (7, 8, 9, 10)

—. _____

_____

—. _____

_____

—. _____

_____

7. Conduct conjoint sessions to assess and reinforce verbalizations of trust toward significant others.

8. Confront irrational belief toward significant other and provide reality-based data to support trust.

9. Encourage client to check out his/her beliefs regarding others by assertively verifying conclusions with others.

10. Use role-playing, behavioral rehearsal, and role reversal to increase client's empathy for others and understanding of the impact of his/her behavior on others.

11. Assess necessity for use of antipsychotic medication to counteract altered thought processes.

12. Arrange for prescription of psychotropic medications by physician.

—. _____

_____

—. _____

_____

—. _____

_____

DIAGNOSTIC SUGGESTIONS

Axis I: 300.23   Social Phobia
310.1   Personality Change Due to (Axis III Disorder)
295.30   Schizophrenia, Paranoid Type
297.1   Delusional Disorder

_____   _____

_____   _____

Axis II: 301.0   Paranoid Personality Disorder
301.22   Schizotypal Personality Disorder

_____   _____

_____   _____

PHOBIA-PANIC/ AGORAPHOBIA

BEHAVIORAL DEFINITIONS

1. A persistent and unreasonable fear of a specific object or situation that promotes avoidance behaviors because an encounter with the phobic stimulus provokes an immediate anxiety response.
2. Unexpected, sudden, debilitating panic symptoms (shallow breathing, sweating, heart racing or pounding, dizziness, depersonalization or derealization, trembling, chest tightness, fear of dying or losing control, nausea) that have occurred repeatedly resulting in persisting concern about having additional attacks or behavioral changes to avoid attacks.
3. Fear of being in an environment that client believes may trigger intense anxiety symptoms (panic) and, therefore, client avoids such situations as leaving home alone, being in a crowd of people, traveling in an enclosed environment.
4. Avoidance or endurance of the phobic stimulus or feared environment with intense anxiety resulting in interference of normal routines or marked distress.
5. Persistence of fear in spite of recognition that the fear is unreasonable.
6. No evidence of agoraphobia.
7. No evidence of panic disorder.

—. _____
   _____
   _____
—. _____
   _____
   _____
—. _____
   _____

LONG-TERM GOALS

1. Reduce fear so that client can independently and freely leave home and comfortably be in public environments.
2. Travel away from home in some form of enclosed transportation.
3. Reduce fear of the specific stimulus object or situation that previously provoked immediate anxiety.
4. Eliminate interference in normal routines and remove distress from feared object or situation.
5. Remove panic symptoms and the fear that they will recur without an ability to cope with and control them.

—. _____
_____
—. _____
_____
—. _____
_____

SHORT-TERM OBJECTIVES

1. Verbalize fear and focus on describing the specific stimuli for it. (1, 9, 10)
2. Construct a hierarchy of situations that increasingly evoke anxiety. (2)
3. Become proficient in progressive, deep-muscle relaxation. (3, 4, 5)
4. Identify a nonthreatening pleasant scene that can be utilized to promote relaxation using guided imagery. (5)

THERAPEUTIC INTERVENTIONS

1. Discuss and assess the fear, its depth, and the stimuli for it.
2. Direct and assist in construction of hierarchy of anxiety-producing situations.
3. Train in progressive relaxation methods.
4. Utilize biofeedback techniques to facilitate relaxation skills.
5. Train in guided imagery for anxiety relief.

The numbers in parentheses accompanying the short-term objectives correspond to the list of suggested therapeutic interventions.

5. Cooperate with systematic desensitization to the anxiety-provoking stimulus object or situation. (5, 6)

6. Undergo in vivo desensitization to the stimulus object or situation. (7)

7. Leave home without overwhelming anxiety. (6, 7, 8, 13)

8. Encounter the phobic stimulus object or situation feeling in control, calm, and comfortable. (1, 7, 8, 13)

9. Identify symbolic significance that the phobic stimulus may have as a basis for fear. (1, 9)

10. Understand the separate realities of the irrationally feared object or situation and the emotionally painful experience from the past that has been evoked by the phobic stimulus. (1, 10, 11, 12)

11. Share the feelings associated with past emotionally painful situation that is connected to the phobia. (9, 10, 11, 12)

12. Differentiate real from distorted, imagined situations that can produce rational and irrational fear. (10, 11, 12)

13. Develop behavioral and cognitive mechanisms that reduce or eliminate irrational anxiety. (3, 5, 7, 13, 15)

6. Direct systematic desensitization procedures to reduce phobic response.

7. Assign and/or accompany client in in vivo desensitization contact with phobic stimulus object or situation.

8. Review and verbally reinforce progress toward overcoming anxiety.

9. Probe, discuss, and interpret possible symbolic meaning to the phobia stimulus object or situation.

10. Clarify and differentiate between the current irrational fear and past emotional pain.

11. Encourage sharing of feelings from past through active listening, positive regard, and questioning.

12. Reinforce insights into past emotional pain and present anxiety.

13. Train in coping strategies (diversion, deep breathing, positive self-talk, muscle relaxation, etc.) to alleviate symptoms.

14. Identify the distorted schemas and related automatic thoughts that mediate anxiety response.

15. Train in revising core schemas using cognitive restructuring techniques.

16. Arrange for the prescription of psychotropic medications to alleviate symptoms.

14. Understand the cognitive beliefs and messages that mediate the anxiety response. (1, 2, 14, 15)

15. Develop positive, healthy, and rational self-talk that reduces fear and allows the behavioral encounter with avoided stimuli. (13, 14, 15)

16. Responsibly take prescribed psychotropic medication to alleviate phobic anxiety. (1, 16)

__. _____

__. _____

__. _____

__. _____

__. _____

__. _____

DIAGNOSTIC SUGGESTIONS

Axis I: 300.01   Panic Disorder without Agoraphobia
300.21   Panic Disorder with Agoraphobia
300.22   Agoraphobia without History of Panic Disorder
300.29   Specific Phobia

_____   _____

_____   _____

PSYCHOTICISM

BEHAVIORAL DEFINITIONS

1. Bizarre content of thought (delusions of grandeur, persecution, reference, influence, control, somatic sensations, or infidelity).
2. Illogical form of thought/speech (loose association of ideas in speech, incoherence; illogical thinking; vague, abstract, or repetitive speech; neologisms, perseverations, clanging).
3. Perception disturbance (hallucinations, primarily auditory but occasionally visual or olfactory).
4. Disturbed affect (blunted, none, flattened, or inappropriate).
5. Lost sense of self (loss of ego boundaries, lack of identify, blatant confusion).
6. Volition diminished (inadequate interest, drive, or ability to follow a course of action to its logical conclusion; pronounced ambivalence or cessation of goal-directed activity).
7. Relationship withdrawal (withdrawal from involvement with external world and preoccupation with egocentric ideas and fantasies, alienation feelings).
8. Psychomotor abnormalities (marked decrease in reactivity to environment; various catatonic patterns such as stupor, rigidity, excitement, posturing, or negativism; unusual mannerisms or grimacing).

—. _____

_____

—. _____

_____

—. _____

_____

LONG-TERM GOALS

1. Control or eliminate active psychotic symptoms such that supervised functioning is positive and medication is taken consistently.
2. Significantly reduce or eliminate hallucinations and/or delusions.
3. Eliminate acute, reactive, psychotic symptoms and return to normal functioning in affect, thinking, and relating.

—. _____

_____

—. _____

_____

—. _____

_____

SHORT-TERM OBJECTIVES

1. Accept and understand that distressing symptoms are due to mental illness. (1, 2, 3, 4)
2. Understand the necessity for taking antipsychotic medications and agree to cooperate with prescribed care. (1, 9, 15, 19)
3. Take antipsychotic medications consistently with or without supervision. (9, 19)
4. Begin to show limited social functioning by responding appropriately to friendly encounters. (4, 5, 7, 11, 15)
5. Think more clearly as demonstrated by logical, coherent speech. (9, 12, 14, 19)

THERAPEUTIC INTERVENTIONS

1. Assess pervasiveness of thought disorder through clinical interview and/or psychological testing.
2. Determine if psychosis is of a brief reactive nature or long term with prodromal and reactive elements.
3. Explore family history for serious mental illness.
4. Provide supportive therapy to alleviate fears and reduce feelings of alienation.
5. Arrange for supervised living situation, if necessary.
6. Probe causes for reactive psychosis.
7. Assist client in reducing threat in the environment.

The numbers in parentheses accompanying the short-term objectives correspond to the list of suggested therapeutic interventions.

6. Report diminishing or absence of hallucinations and/or delusions. (8, 9, 10, 12)

7. Gradually return to premorbid level of functioning and accept responsibility of caring for own basic needs. (6, 15, 19, 20)

8. Verbalize an understanding of the underlying needs, conflicts, and emotions that support the irrational beliefs. (6, 10, 11, 12, 13)

9. Increase family's positive support of client to reduce chances of acute exacerbation of psychotic episode. (16, 17, 18)

—. _____
   _____

—. _____
   _____

—. _____
   _____

8. Explore feelings surrounding stressors that triggered psychotic episodes.

9. Arrange for administration of appropriate psychotropic medications through a physician.

10. Assist in restructuring irrational beliefs by reviewing reality-based evidence and misinterpretation.

11. Differentiate for client the source of stimuli between self-generated messages and reality of external world.

12. Encourage focus on the reality of external world versus the client's distorted fantasy.

13. Probe the underlying needs and feelings (e.g., inadequacy, rejection, anxiety, guilt).

14. Gently confront illogical thoughts and speech to refocus disordered thinking.

15. Demonstrate acceptance through calm, nurturing manner, good eye contact, and active listening.

16. Arrange family therapy sessions to educate regarding client's illness, treatment, and prognosis.

17. Encourage family members to share their feelings of frustration, guilt, fear, or depression surrounding client's mental illness and behavior patterns.

18. Assist family in avoiding double-bind messages that increase anxiety and psychotic symptoms in client.

19. Monitor client for medication compliance and redirect if client is noncompliant.

20. Monitor client's daily level of functioning—that is, reality orientation, personal hygiene, social interactions, affect appropriateness—and give feedback that either redirects or reinforces client's progress.

—. _____
   _____

—. _____
   _____

—. _____
   _____

DIAGNOSTIC SUGGESTIONS

Axis I:	297.1	Delusional Disorder
	298.8	Brief Psychotic Disorder
	295.xx	Schizophrenia
	295.30	Schizophrenia, Paranoid Type
	295.70	Schizoaffective Disorder
	295.40	Schizophreniform Disorder
	296.xx	Bipolar I Disorder
	296.89	Bipolar II Disorder
	296.xx	Major Depressive Disorder
	310.1	Personality Change Due to (Axis III Disorder)
	_____	_____
	_____	_____

SEXUAL ABUSE

BEHAVIORAL DEFINITIONS

1. Vague memories that indicate inappropriate childhood sexual contact that can be corroborated by significant others.
2. Self-report of being sexually abused.
3. Inability to recall years of childhood.
4. Extreme difficulty becoming intimate with others.
5. Inability to enjoy sexual contact with a desired partner.
6. Unexplainable feelings of anger, rage, or fear when coming into contact with a close family relative.
7. Pervasive pattern of promiscuity or the sexualization of relationships.

—. _____

_____

—. _____

_____

—. _____

_____

LONG-TERM GOALS

1. Resolve the issue of being sexually abused with an increased capacity for intimacy in relationships.
2. Begin the healing process from sexual abuse with resultant enjoyment of appropriate sexual contact.
3. Work successfully through the issues related to being sexually abused with consequent understanding and control of feelings.
4. Recognize and accept the sexual abuse without inappropriate sexualization of relationships.
5. Establish whether or not sexual abuse occurred.

6. Begin the process of moving away from being a victim of sexual abuse and toward becoming a survivor of sexual abuse.

—. _____

—. _____

—. _____

SHORT-TERM OBJECTIVES

1. Tell the entire story of the abuse. (1, 2, 3, 11)
2. Identify the nature, frequency, and duration of the abuse. (1, 2, 3, 13)
3. Identify and express the feelings connected to the abuse. (2, 4, 5, 13)
4. Decrease the secrecy in the family by informing key members regarding the abuse. (1, 8, 9, 11)
5. Clarify memories of the abuse. (1, 3, 8, 15)
6. Develop a support system of key individuals who will be encouraging and helpful in aiding the process of resolving the issue. (10, 17)
7. Increase knowledge of sexual abuse and its effect. (12, 13, 14, 16)

THERAPEUTIC INTERVENTIONS

1. Actively build level of trust with client in session to help increase ability to self-disclose.
2. Explore, encourage, and support client in verbally expressing and clarifying feelings associated with the abuse.
3. Ask client to draw a diagram of house in which he/she was raised, complete with where everyone slept, and share it with therapist.
4. Guide the client in an empty chair exercise with a key figure connected to the abuse—that is, perpetrator, sibling, parent.
5. Assign client to write a letter to the perpetrator and process it with therapist.
6. Assign client to write an angry letter to the perpetra-

The numbers in parentheses accompanying the short-term objectives correspond to the list of suggested therapeutic interventions.

8. Verbalize the ways the sexual abuse has impacted his/her life. (2, 13, 16, 17)

9. Decrease statements of being a victim while increasing statements that reflect personal empowerment. (7, 16, 17, 18)

10. Increase ability to talk openly about the abuse, reflecting acceptance of the abuse. (1, 8, 11, 17)

11. Increase level of forgiveness of self, perpetrator, and others connected with the abuse. (4, 6, 7, 16)

12. Identify the positive aspects for self of being able to forgive all those involved with the abuse. (7, 13, 16, 18)

13. Verbally identify self as a survivor of sexual abuse. (12, 13, 17, 18)

14. Decrease feelings of shame by being able to verbally affirm self as not responsible for abuse. (12, 13, 16, 17)

15. Decrease emotional intensity of the feelings connected to the abuse. (2, 4, 5, 6)

16. Increase level of trust of others as shown by more socialization and greater intimacy tolerance. (10, 11, 17)

tor and process it with therapist.

7. Assign client to write a forgiveness letter and/or complete a forgiveness exercise and process each with therapist.

8. Facilitate conjoint session with client and parents assisting and supporting them in revealing the abuse.

9. Hold conjoint session where client confronts the perpetrator of the abuse.

10. Teach the client the share-check method of building trust in relationships.

11. Hold conjoint session where client tells spouse of the abuse.

12. Assign and process written exercise in *The Courage to Heal Workbook* (Davis).

13. Assign client to read chapter or section in the books *The Courage to Heal* (Bass and Davis); *Betrayal of Innocence* (Forward and Buck); *Outgrowing the Pain* (Gil); and process key concepts with therapist.

14. Develop with client a genogram and assist in illuminating key family patterns of sexual boundaries and intimacy.

15. Develop with client a symptom line connected to the abuse.

16. Assign client to read sections in *Healing the Shame*

—. _____
    _____
—. _____
    _____
—. _____
    _____

That Binds You (Bradshaw); *Shame* (Kaufman); *Facing Shame* (Fossum and Mason); and process key concepts with therapist.

17. Encourage client to attend a support group for survivors of sexual abuse.

18. Ask client to complete an exercise that identifies the positives and negatives of being a victim and the positives and negatives of being a survivor. Compare and process lists with therapist.

—. _____
    _____
—. _____
    _____
—. _____
    _____

DIAGNOSTIC SUGGESTIONS

Axis I:	303.90	Alcohol Dependence
	304.80	Polysubstance Dependence
	300.4	Dysthymic Disorder
	296.xx	Major Depressive Disorder
	300.02	Generalized Anxiety Disorder
	300.14	Dissociative Identity Disorder
	300.15	Dissociative Disorder NOS
	V61.21	Sexual Abuse of Child (995.53, Victim)
	_____	_____
	_____	_____
Axis II:	301.82	Avoidant Personality Disorder
	301.6	Dependent Personality Disorder
	_____	_____
	_____	_____

SLEEP DISTURBANCE

BEHAVIORAL DEFINITIONS

1. Difficulty getting to or maintaining sleep.
2. Sleeping adequately but not feeling refreshed or rested after waking.
3. Predominant daytime sleepiness or falling asleep too easily during daytime.
4. Insomnia or hypersomnia complaints due to a reversal of the sleep-wake schedule normal for the patient's environment.
5. Distress resulting from repeated awakening with detailed recall of extremely frightening dreams involving threats to self.
6. Abrupt awakening with a panicky scream followed by intense anxiety and autonomic arousal, no detailed dream recall, and confusion or disorientation.
7. Repeated incidents of sleepwalking accompanied by amnesia for the episode.

—. _____
   _____
—. _____
   _____
—. _____
   _____

LONG-TERM GOALS

1. Restore restful sleep pattern.
2. Feel refreshed and energetic during wakeful hours.
3. Terminate anxiety-producing dreams that cause awakening.
4. End abrupt awakening in terror and return to peaceful, restful sleep pattern.
5. Restore restful sleep with reduction of sleepwalking incidents.

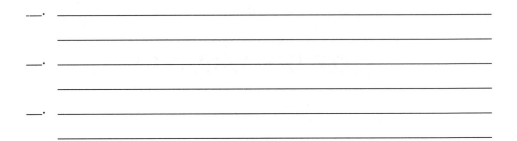

SHORT-TERM OBJECTIVES

1. Keep a journal of daily stressors and sleep pattern. (1, 2, 3, 4)

2. Share history of substance abuse or medication use. (2)

3. Verbalize depressive feelings and share possible causes. (1, 2, 3)

4. Discuss experiences of emotional traumas that continue to disturb sleep. (1, 4, 12, 13)

5. Follow sleep induction schedule of events. (5)

6. Practice deep-muscle relaxation exercises. (6)

7. Utilize biofeedback training to deepen relaxation skill. (7)

8. Keep physician appointment to assess organic contributions to sleep disorder. (8, 14)

9. Describe disturbing dreams by keeping a dream journal. (9, 11)

THERAPEUTIC INTERVENTIONS

1. Assign client to keep a journal of daily stressors and nightly sleep patterns.

2. Assess contribution of medication or substance abuse to sleep disorder.

3. Assess role of depression as cause of sleep disturbance.

4. Explore recent traumatic events that interfere with sleep.

5. Assign adherence to a strict sleep induction routine, daily exercise, low stimulation prior to sleep, relaxation training, bland diet, and so forth.

6. Train in deep-muscle relaxation exercises with and without audio tape instruction.

7. Administer electromyographic (EMG) biofeedback to reinforce successful relaxation response.

The numbers in parentheses accompanying the short-term objectives correspond to the list of suggested therapeutic interventions.

10. Take antidepressant medication daily for 3 weeks to assess effect on sleep. (10, 15)

11. Discuss fears regarding relinquishing control. (4, 11, 12, 13)

12. Share childhood traumatic experiences associated with sleep experience. (4, 12)

13. Reveal sexual abuse incidents that continue to be disturbing. (4, 12, 13)

14. Cooperate with sleep clinic referral and evaluation. (14)

—. _____
   _____

—. _____
   _____

—. _____
   _____

8. Refer to physician to rule out physical and pharmacological causes for sleep disturbance.

9. Probe nature of disturbing dreams and relationship to life stress. Assign client to keep a dream journal.

10. Arrange for antidepressant medication to enhance restful sleep.

11. Probe fears related to letting go of control.

12. Explore traumas of childhood that surround the sleep experience.

13. Explore possible sexual abuse that has not been revealed.

14. Refer to sleep clinic for assessment of sleep apnea or other physiological factors.

15. Monitor client for medication compliance and effectiveness.

—. _____
   _____

—. _____
   _____

—. _____
   _____

DIAGNOSTIC SUGGESTIONS

Axis I: 307.42   Primary Insomnia
307.44   Primary Hypersomnia
307.45   Circadian Rhythm Sleep Disorder
307.47   Nightmare Disorder
307.46   Sleep Terror Disorder
307.46   Sleepwalking Disorder
309.81   Posttraumatic Stress Disorder
296.xx   Major Depressive Disorder
300.4   Dysthymic Disorder

_____   _____

_____   _____

SOCIAL DISCOMFORT

BEHAVIORAL DEFINITIONS

1. Overall pattern of social anxiety, shyness, or timidity that presents itself in most social situations.
2. Hypersensitivity to the criticism or disapproval of others.
3. No close friends or confidants outside of first-degree relatives.
4. Avoidance of situations that require a degree of interpersonal contact.
5. Reluctant involvement in social situations out of fear of saying or doing something foolish or of becoming emotional in front of others.
6. Abuse of alcohol or chemical to help ease the anxiety of becoming involved in social situations.
7. Isolation during most waking hours or involvement in solitary activities.
8. Increased heart rate, sweating, dry mouth, muscle tension, and shakiness in most social situations.

LONG-TERM GOALS

1. Interact socially without excessive fear or anxiety.
2. Develop the essential social skills that will enhance the quality of relationship life.

3. Develop the ability to form relationships that will enhance recovery support system.
4. Reach a personal balance between solitary time and interpersonal interaction with others.

—. _____

_____

—. _____

_____

—. _____

_____

SHORT-TERM OBJECTIVES

1. Initiate one social contact per day for increasing lengths of time. (1, 2, 4)
2. Identify and clarify nature of fears connected to associating with others. (2, 5, 6, 8)
3. Identify how shame affects relating with others. (6, 8)
4. Describe positive feelings associated with contact and involvement with others. (1, 3, 7)
5. Identify sources of low self-esteem in childhood experiences. (5, 6, 8)
6. Identify sources of fear of rejection in childhood experiences. (5, 6, 8)
7. Increase length and frequency of contact with others. (1, 3, 4, 11)

THERAPEUTIC INTERVENTIONS

1. Assign client to initiate one 5-minute conversation daily and report results to therapist.
2. Assist client in identifying fears tied to relating with others and in developing strategies for overcoming them.
3. Ask client to attend and participate in available social and recreational activities within treatment program or the community.
4. Monitor, encourage, redirect, and give feedback to client as necessary relating to his/her interaction with others.
5. Probe childhood experiences of criticism, abandonment, or abuse that would foster low self-esteem and shame.

The numbers in parentheses accompanying the short-term objectives correspond to the list of suggested therapeutic interventions.

8. Verbally report positive outcomes of participation in social and support groups. (3, 11, 15)

9. Participate verbally in a meaningful way in group therapy. (4, 7, 9)

10. Verbally report and demonstrate a renewed sense of trust in others. (3, 7, 17)

11. Participate in a designated amount of activities provided within the treatment setting. (3, 4, 11, 12)

12. Increase assertiveness skills. (9)

13. Develop a positive self-talk dialogue that will help overcome fear of interacting with others. (10, 13)

14. Recall past positive experiences of being involved in social activities and/or relating one-on-one with others. (18)

15. Identify ways he/she is like other people and therefore acceptable to others. (16, 17)

16. Develop a written plan that divides non-workdays between social and solitary activities. (14)

17. Verbally describe the defense mechanisms used to avoid close relationships. (15, 16, 17)

6. Explore childhood and adolescent experiences of rejection and neglect that would foster fear of rejection.

7. Assign client to self-disclose two times in each group therapy session.

8. Assign client to read the books *Healing the Shame That Binds You* (Bradshaw); *Facing Shame* (Fossum and Mason); and process key concepts with therapist.

9. Train client in assertiveness skills or refer to an assertiveness-training class.

10. Refer client to attend a communication improvement seminar or a Dale Carnegie course.

11. Encourage and support client in his/her effort to initiate and build social relationships.

12. Facilitate a role-play with client around initiating a conversation with another person for the first time. Process the experience with client afterward.

13. Assist client in developing self-talk that will aid in overcoming fear of relating with others or participating in social activities.

14. Ask client to develop a daily plan for nonworking hours that contains both social and solitary activities. Review plan and give feedback.

___. _____
    _____
___. _____
    _____
___. _____
    _____

15. Refer client to self-help group (i.e., AA, NA, Emotions Anonymous, or Recovery Inc.) and process the experience with therapist.

16. Assist client in recognizing how he/she is like or similar to others.

17. Assist client in identifying defense mechanisms that keep others at a distance and in finding ways to keep defensiveness level at a minimum.

18. Ask client to list and process positive experiences from social activities.

___. _____
    _____
___. _____
    _____
___. _____
    _____

DIAGNOSTIC SUGGESTIONS

Axis I: 300.23   Social Phobia
              300.4   Dysthymic Disorder
              296.xx   Major Depressive Disorder
              300.21   Panic Disorder with Agoraphobia
              309.81   Posttraumatic Stress Disorder

              _____   _____
              _____   _____

Axis II: 301.82   Avoidant Personality Disorder
              301.20   Schizoid Personality Disorder
              301.0   Paranoid Personality Disorder
              301.22   Schizotypal Personality Disorder

              _____   _____
              _____   _____

SOMATIZATION

BEHAVIORAL DEFINITIONS

1. Preoccupation with some imagined defect in appearance or excessive concern regarding a small abnormality.
2. A physical malady caused by a psychosocial stressor triggering a psychological conflict.
3. Preoccupation with the fear of having a serious physical disease without any medical basis for concern.
4. A multitude of physical complaints that have no organic foundation and have caused the client to change his/her life (e.g., see doctors often, take prescriptions, withdraw from responsibilities).
5. Preoccupation with chronic pain grossly beyond what is expected for a physical malady or in spite of no known organic cause.
6. One or more physical complaints (usually vague) that have no known organic basis, or the complaining and impairment in life functioning in excess of what is expected.
7. Preoccupation with pain in one or more anatomical sites with both psychological factors and a medical condition as a basis for the pain.

__. _____
   _____
__. _____
   _____
__. _____
   _____

LONG-TERM GOALS

1. Reduce frequency of physical complaints and improve the level of independent functioning.
2. Reduce verbalizations focusing on pain while increasing productive activities.
3. Accept body appearance as normal even with insignificant flaws.
4. Accept self as relatively healthy with no known medical illness.
5. Improve physical functioning due to development of adequate coping mechanisms for stress management.

—. _____

_____

_____

—. _____

_____

_____

—. _____

_____

SHORT-TERM OBJECTIVES

1. Verbalize negative feeling regarding body and discuss self-prediction of catastrophized consequences of perceived body abnormality. (1, 2)
2. Identify the connection between negative body image and general low self-esteem. (2, 3)
3. List causes for feelings of low self-esteem and inadequacy based in early family history. (3, 4, 5)

THERAPEUTIC INTERVENTIONS

1. Listen to client's initial complaints without rejection or confrontation.
2. Refocus client's discussion from physical complaints to emotional conflicts and expression of feelings.
3. Explore sources of emotional pain; feelings of fear, inadequacy, rejection, or abuse.
4. Explore family history of reinforcement of physical complaints.

The numbers in parentheses accompanying the short-term objectives correspond to the list of suggested therapeutic interventions.

4. Focus attention and energy on other people and activities rather than self and physical complaints. (6, 8, 13)

5. Understand and verbalize the secondary gain that results from physical complaints. (12, 16)

6. Identify family patterns that exist around exaggerated focus on physical maladies. (3, 4, 5)

7. Verbalize acceptance of body as normal in function and appearance. (10, 11, 15)

8. Decrease physical complaints and increase verbal assessment of self as able to function normally and productively. (7, 9, 12, 15)

9. Develop coping mechanisms for stress that are more constructive—that is, exercise, relaxation, diversion activities, assertiveness, socialization, project completion. (6, 8, 9, 15)

10. Develop alternative coping strategies versus doctoring and medication. (2, 6, 8, 9)

11. Accept referral to a pain clinic to learn pain management techniques. (17)

12. Discuss causes for emotional stress in life that underlie the focus on physical complaints. (3, 7, 14)

5. Probe causes for low self-esteem and fears of inadequacy in childhood experiences.

6. Assign diversion activities that take focus off self and redirect toward hobby, social activities, assisting others, completing projects, returning to work.

7. Assist client in acceptance of connection between physical focus and avoidance of facing emotional conflicts.

8. Assign client to develop a list of pleasurable activities that can serve as rewards and diversions from bodily focus.

9. Train client in relaxation techniques.

10. Train in assertiveness or refer to an assertiveness-training class.

11. Reinforce assertiveness as means of attaining healthy need satisfaction in contrast to whining helplessness.

12. Give positive feedback when client is symptom-free.

13. Discuss the destructive social impact on friends and family of consistent verbalization of negative body focus.

14. Discuss causes for anger and means of healthy anger expression.

13. Engage in normal responsibilities vocationally and
socially without withdrawal
into avoidance using physical complaint focus as
excuse. (6, 12, 13)

___. _____
_____

___. _____
_____

___. _____
_____

15. Empower client to take
control of his/her environment rather than continue
helpless frustration, anger,
and "poor me."

16. Assist client in developing
insight into the secondary
gain received from physical
illness, complaints, and the
like.

17. Ask client to complete an
assessment at a pain clinic.

___. _____
_____
_____

___. _____
_____
_____

___. _____
_____

DIAGNOSTIC SUGGESTIONS

Axis I:	300.7	Body Dysmorphic Disorder
	300.11	Conversion Disorder
	300.7	Hypochondriasis
	300.81	Somatization Disorder
	307.80	Pain Disorder Associated with Psychological Factors
	307.89	Pain Disorder Associated with Psychological Factors and (Axis III Disorder)
	300.82	Undifferentiated Somatoform Disorder
	300.4	Dysthymic Disorder
	_____	_____
	_____	_____

SPIRITUAL CONFUSION

BEHAVIORAL DEFINITIONS

1. Verbalization of a desire for a closer relationship to a higher power but with difficulty.
2. A struggle with Alcoholics Anonymous (AA) Steps 2 and 3 and difficulty in believing in a higher power.
3. Feelings and attitudes about higher power that are characterized by fear, anger, and distrust.
4. Verbalizes a feeling of emptiness in his/her life, as if something were missing.

—. _____
   _____

—. _____
   _____

LONG-TERM GOALS

1. Clarify spiritual concepts and instill a freedom to approach a higher power as a resource for support.
2. Increase belief in and development of relationship with a higher power.
3. Begin a faith in a higher power and incorporate it into a support system.

—. _____
   _____

—. _____
   _____

SHORT-TERM OBJECTIVES

1. Describe beliefs around the idea of a higher power. (1, 4, 7)

2. Verbalize an increase in level of acceptance and forgiveness for self. (2, 3, 9)

3. Increase knowledge and understanding of concept of a higher power. (2, 3, 4, 6)

4. Identify and verbalize feelings related to a higher power. (4, 6, 8, 9)

5. Verbalize acceptance of forgiveness from a higher power. (2, 3, 4)

6. Replace concept of higher power as harsh and judgmental with one where higher power is accepting, forgiving, and loving. (2, 5, 9, 10)

—. _____
   _____

—. _____
   _____

—. _____
   _____

THERAPEUTIC INTERVENTIONS

1. Assist in processing ideas and feelings regarding a higher power in group and individual sessions.

2. Ask client to read the books *Serenity* (Helmfelt and Fowler)—all readings related to AA Steps 2 and 3; *The Road Less Traveled* (Peck); and *Search for Serenity* (Presnall).

3. Ask client to talk with chaplains regarding spiritual struggle and record their feedback.

4. Assign a list of all beliefs related to a higher power and process it with the client in an individual session.

5. Assist in implementing daily meditation and/or prayer and report results to therapist.

6. Ask client to make a chart of advantages and disadvantages regarding his/her belief in a higher power.

7. Review early life experiences surrounding belief in higher power.

8. Explore religious distortions and judgementalism that client was subjected to by others.

The numbers in parentheses accompanying the short-term objectives correspond to the list of suggested therapeutic interventions.

9. Explore feelings of shame and guilt that led to feeling unworthy to higher power and others.

10. Assist in evaluating religious tenets separated from painful emotional experience with religious people in client's past.

___. _____

_____

___. _____

_____

___. _____

_____

DIAGNOSTIC SUGGESTIONS

Axis I:

300.4	Dysthymic Disorder
311	Depressive Disorder NOS
300.00	Anxiety Disorder NOS
296.xx	Major Depressive Disorder
_____	_____
_____	_____

SUICIDAL IDEATION

BEHAVIORAL DEFINITIONS

1. Recurrent thoughts of or preoccupation with death.
2. Recurrent or ongoing suicidal ideation without any plans.
3. Ongoing suicidal ideation with a specific plan.
4. Recent suicide attempt.
5. Past history of suicide attempts that required professional or family/friend intervention on some level (i.e., inpatient, safe house, outpatient, supervision).
6. A positive family history of suicide and preoccupation with suicide thoughts.
7. A bleak, hopeless attitude regarding life coupled with recent life events that support this (i.e., divorce, death, loss of job).
8. Sudden change from being depressed to upbeat and at peace while actions indicate client is "putting his/her house in order" and there has been no genuine resolution of conflict issues.

—. _____
   _____
—. _____
   _____
—. _____
   _____

LONG-TERM GOALS

1. Alleviate suicidal impulses/ideation and return to highest level of previous daily functioning.
2. Stabilize suicidal crisis.

3. Place client in appropriate level of care to address suicidal crisis.
4. Reestablish a sense of hope for self and life.

—. _____

_____

—. _____

_____

—. _____

_____

SHORT-TERM OBJECTIVES

1. Identify life factors that preceded the suicidal ideation. (7, 8, 14)

2. Report no longer feeling the impulse to take his/her life. (2, 7, 11, 12)

3. Report a decrease in the frequency and intensity of the suicidal ideation. (2, 8, 9, 13)

4. Reestablish a consistent eating and sleeping pattern. (10, 12)

5. Express, with appropriate affect, feelings that underlie suicide ideation. (7, 8, 13, 14)

6. Discuss suicidal feelings, thoughts, and plans. (1, 2, 3, 5, 9)

7. Identify positive things in his/her life. (11)

THERAPEUTIC INTERVENTIONS

1. Assess suicidal ideation taking into account extent of ideation, the presence of a primary and back-up plan, past attempts, and family history. Then make appropriate intervention or referral.

2. Assess and monitor suicidal potential on an ongoing basis.

3. Notify family and significant others of the suicidal ideation. Ask them to form a 24-hour suicide watch until the crisis subsides.

4. Assist client in developing an awareness of his/her cognitive messages that reinforce hopelessness and helplessness.

5. Draw up a contract with client identifying what he/she will do when experiencing suicidal thoughts or impulses.

The numbers in parentheses accompanying the short-term objectives correspond to the list of suggested therapeutic interventions.

8. Verbally report and demonstrate an increased sense of hope for self. (2, 4, 11)

9. Report suicidal impulses to a designated significant other or helping professional. (2, 3, 6)

10. Take medications as prescribed and report all side effects. (2, 6)

11. Sign and follow all the stipulations in the suicide contract. (2, 5)

12. Follow through with all of the professional recommendations for the suicidal crisis. (3, 5, 6, 10, 12)

—. _____

   _____

—. _____

   _____

—. _____

   _____

6. Monitor client for effect of and compliance with prescribed medication. Confer with prescribing physician on a regular basis.

7. Explore sources of emotional pain and hopelessness.

8. Encourage client to express feelings related to suicidal ideation in order to clarify them and increase insight as to the causes.

9. Arrange for client to take Minnesota Multiphasic Personality Inventory (MMPI) or Beck Depression Inventory (BDI) and evaluate results for degree of depression.

10. Arrange for hospitalization when client is judged to be harmful to self.

11. Assist client in finding positive, hopeful things in his/her life at the present time.

12. Assist client in developing coping strategies for suicidal ideation (e.g., more physical exercise, less internal focus, increased social involvement, and more expression of feelings).

13. Develop a penitence ritual for client with suicidal ideation connected with being a survivor and implement it with him/her.

14. Assist client in becoming aware of life factors that were significant precursors to the beginning of his/her suicidal ideation.

—. _____

_____

—. _____

_____

—. _____

_____

DIAGNOSTIC SUGGESTIONS

Axis I: 296.xx Bipolar I Disorder
300.4 Dysthymic Disorder
296.2x Major Depressive Disorder, Single Episode
296.3x Major Depressive Disorder, Recurrent
296.89 Bipolar II Disorder

_____ _____

_____ _____

Axis II: 301.83 Borderline Personality Disorder

_____ _____

_____ _____

TYPE A BEHAVIOR

BEHAVIORAL DEFINITIONS

1. A pattern of pressuring self and others to accomplish more because there is never enough time.
2. A spirit of intense competition in all activities.
3. Intense compulsion to win at all costs regardless of the activity or co-competitor.
4. Inclination to dominate all social or business situations, being too direct and overbearing.
5. Propensity to become irritated by the action of others who do not conform to client's sense of propriety or correctness.
6. A state of perpetual impatience with any waiting, delays, or interruptions.
7. Difficulty in sitting or doing nothing.
8. Psychomotor facial signs such as hostility, tension, or tics.
9. Psychomotor voice signs such as irritatingly forceful speech or laughter, rapid and intense speech, and frequent use of obscenities.

—. _____
_____
—. _____
_____
—. _____
_____

LONG-TERM GOALS

1. Begin to formulate and implement a new life attitudinal pattern that allows for a more relaxed pattern of living.

2. Reach a balance between work/competitive and social/noncompetitive time in daily life.
3. Achieve an overall decrease in compulsive, driven behaviors.
4. Begin to develop daily social and recreational routines.
5. Alleviate sense of time urgency, free-floating anxiety, and self-destructive behaviors.

—. _____

_____

—. _____

_____

—. _____

_____

SHORT-TERM OBJECTIVES

1. Practice deep-muscle relaxation to relieve tension and slow pace of life. (1)
2. Verbalize distinction between respectful assertiveness and insensitive directness or verbal aggression that is controlling. (2, 6)
3. Identify specifically the beliefs that support driven, overachieving behavior. (4, 6, 21)
4. Identify pattern of trying unsuccessfully to please a parent figure since childhood. (3, 4, 21)
5. Identify role models that foster a driven lifestyle. (3, 4)

THERAPEUTIC INTERVENTIONS

1. Train client in deep-muscle relaxation and breathing exercises to slow pace of life.
2. Train client in assertiveness to learn to avoid aggression and trampling on rights of others.
3. Assign client to read the books *Positive Addiction* (Glasser) and *Overdoing It* (Robinson) and select key ideas to discuss with therapist.
4. Probe family of origin history for role models of high achievement and compulsive drive.

The numbers in parentheses accompanying the short-term objectives correspond to the list of suggested therapeutic interventions.

6. Increase interest in the lives of others as evidenced by listening to others talk of their life experiences. (7, 18)

7. Decrease number of hours worked daily and taking work home. (3, 5, 16)

8. Develop the ability to analyze his/her dreams. (11, 12)

9. Show verbal recognition of hostility toward and impatience with others. (2, 6, 7, 9)

10. Identify the sources of hostility. (9)

11. Increase daily time involved in relaxing activities. (5, 10, 16, 17)

12. Demonstrate increased interest in activities other than vocational. (5, 10, 13, 16)

13. Develop an internal monitor to balance daily activities of work and leisure. (3, 8, 14, 15)

14. Demonstrate increased ability to give and receive love by being more affectionate physically and verbally. (7, 8, 13, 14)

15. Develop pattern of doing one task at a time with less emphasis on pressure to complete it quickly. (3, 8, 14, 19)

5. Assign client to do one noncompetitive, recreational activity each day for a week and process this experience with therapist.

6. Ask client to make a list of his/her beliefs about self-worth and the worth of others. Process it with therapist.

7. Confront and reframe client's actions or verbalizations when he/she is self-centered or reflects a lack of feeling for others.

8. Train client in self-talk that will assist in altering beliefs that foster the compulsive behaviors.

9. Reflect client's hostility and assist in identifying its source.

10. Ask client to read biographies or autobiographies of people (St. Augustine, Thomas Merton, Albert Schweitzer, C. S. Lewis, etc.) and process the key beliefs they lived by with therapist.

11. Assign client to keep a daily dream journal.

12. Help the client develop the ability to analyze his/her dreams.

13. Assign client to read the book *The Road Less Traveled* (Peck) and process key ideas with therapist.

16. Verbalize decreased impatience with others by talking of appreciating and understanding the good qualities of others. (6, 7, 10, 18)

17. Identify the positive aspects of employing understanding, compassion, and forgiveness in dealing with others. (2, 3, 6, 10)

18. Develop a daily routine that reflects a balance between the quest for achievement and appreciation of aesthetic things. (5, 10, 13, 20)

19. Verbalize self-talk that is not self-centered in nature or content. (8)

20. Increase listening to others in conversation. (2, 7, 18)

—. _____
_____

—. _____
_____

—. _____
_____

14. Reinforce all client changes that reflect a greater sense of life balance.

15. Assist client in identifying the beliefs he/she lives by and connecting them to behavior patterns in daily life.

16. Ask client to try one area of interest outside of his/her vocation that he/she will do two times weekly for one month.

17. Assign client to watch comedy movies and identify the positive aspects of them with therapist.

18. Assign client to talk to an associate or child, focusing on listening to the other person and learning several key things about that person.

19. Give client an Ericksonian assignment—that is, at a certain time drive __ miles exactly, stop, pull over, and think about _____ for __ minutes, then return and process assignment with therapist.

20. Assign client to read "List of Aphorisms" in *Treating Type A Behaviors and Your Heart* (Friedman and Olmer) three times daily for one or two weeks; then pick several to incorporate into his/her life.

21. Probe family of origin for history of being pressured to achieve but never succeeding at satisfying parent figure.

—. _____
   _____

—. _____
   _____

—. _____
   _____

DIAGNOSTIC SUGGESTIONS

Axis I: 300.3   Obsessive-Compulsive Disorder
             300.02   Generalized Anxiety Disorder

             _____   _____
             _____   _____

Axis II: 301.4   Obsessive-Compulsive Personality Disorder

             _____   _____
             _____   _____

VOCATIONAL STRESS

BEHAVIORAL DEFINITIONS

1. Feelings of anxiety and depression secondary to interpersonal conflict (perceived harassment, shunning, confrontation, etc.) with co-workers.
2. Feelings of inadequacy, fear, and failure secondary to severe business losses.
3. Fear of failure secondary to success or promotion that increases perceived expectations for greater success.
4. Rebellion against and/or conflicts with authority figures in the employment situation.
5. Feelings of anxiety and depression secondary to being fired or laid off resulting in unemployment.
6. Anxiety related to perceived or actual job jeopardy due.
7. Feelings of depression and anxiety related to complaints of job dissatisfaction or stress of the employment responsibilities.

—. _____
   _____
—. _____
   _____
—. _____
   _____

LONG-TERM GOALS

1. Improve satisfaction and comfort surrounding co-worker relationships.
2. Increase sense of confidence and competence in dealing with work responsibilities.

3. Be cooperative with and accepting of supervision or direction in the work setting.
4. Increase sense of self-esteem and elevation of mood in spite of unemployment.
5. Increase job security as a result of more positive evaluation of performance by supervisor.
6. Engage in job-seeking behaviors consistently and with a reasonably positive attitude.
7. Increase job satisfaction and performance due to implementation of assertiveness and stress management strategies.

—. _____
_____
—. _____
_____
—. _____
_____

SHORT-TERM OBJECTIVES

1. Describe nature of conflicts with co-workers or supervisor. (1, 2, 3, 13)
2. Identify client's role in the conflict with co-workers or supervisor. (1, 2, 16, 17)
3. Identify behavioral changes client could make in interaction to help resolve conflict with co-workers or supervisors. (1, 2, 18)
4. Identify patterns of similar conflict with people outside of work environment. (3, 4)
5. Review family of origin history to determine roots

THERAPEUTIC INTERVENTIONS

1. Clarify the nature of conflicts in work setting.
2. Confront projection of responsibility for client's behavior and feelings onto others.
3. Discuss possible patterns of interpersonal conflict that occur beyond the work setting.
4. Probe family of origin history for causes of current interpersonal conflict patterns.
5. Probe childhood history for roots of feelings of inadequacy, fear of failure, or fear of success.

The numbers in parentheses accompanying the short-term objectives correspond to the list of suggested therapeutic interventions.

for interpersonal conflict that are being reenacted in the work atmosphere. (4)

6. Review family of origin history to find roots of feelings of inadequacy, fear of failure, or fear of success. (5, 6)

7. Verbalize feelings of fear, anger, and helplessness associated with the vocational stress. (6, 7, 8)

8. Identify distorted cognitive messages associated with perception of job stress. (7, 8, 10)

9. Develop more healthy, realistic cognitive messages that promote harmony with others, self-acceptance, and self-confidence. (8, 10)

10. Replace projection of responsibility for conflict, feelings, or behavior with acceptance of responsibility for behavior, feelings, and role in conflict. (2, 9)

11. Verbalize an understanding of circumstances that led up to being terminated from employment. (1, 10, 11, 12)

12. Cease self-disparaging comments that are based on perceived failure at employment. (5, 8, 11, 12, 18)

13. Develop assertiveness skills that allow for effective communication of needs and feelings without aggression or defensiveness. (3, 13, 14)

6. Probe and clarify emotions surrounding the vocational stress.

7. Assess the cognitive messages and schema connected with vocational stress.

8. Train in the development of more realistic, healthy cognitive messages that relieve anxiety and depression.

9. Reinforce acceptance of responsibility for personal feelings and behavior.

10. Confront catastrophizing the situation leading to immobilizing anxiety.

11. Probe causes for termination of employment or job jeopardy that may have been beyond the client's control.

12. Reinforce realistic self-appraisal of client's successes and failures at employment.

13. Train in assertiveness skills or refer to assertiveness-training class.

14. Use role-playing, behavioral rehearsal, and role-reversal to increase the probability of positive encounters and reduce anxiety with others in employment situation or job search.

15. Assign client to write a plan for constructive action that contains various alternatives.

16. Explore possible role of substance abuse in vocational conflicts.

17. Explore the transfer of other personal problems to the employment situation.

14. Rehearse interpersonal behaviors that will promote harmony with co-workers and supervisors. (1, 14, 15)

15. Develop and verbalize plan for constructive action to reduce vocational stress. (7, 15)

16. Review success in all areas of life that affirm self as capable and likable. (8, 11, 12)

17. Outline plan for job search. (19, 20, 21)

18. Report on job search experiences and feelings surrounding these experiences. (22)

18. Explore the effect of vocational stress on intra- and interpersonal dynamics.

19. Help client develop a written job plan that contains specific obtainable objectives for job search.

20. Assign client to choose jobs in want ads and ask friends or family about job opportunities.

21. Assign client to attend a job search class or resume-writing seminar.

22. Monitor and process client's search for employment.

—. _____

    _____

—. _____

    _____

—. _____

    _____

—. _____

    _____

—. _____

    _____

—. _____

    _____

DIAGNOSTIC SUGGESTIONS

Axis I:	309.0	Adjustment Disorder with Depressed Mood
	300.4	Dysthymic Disorder
	296.xx	Major Depressive Disorder
	V62.2	Occupational Problem
	309.24	Adjustment Disorder with Anxiety
	303.90	Alcohol Dependence
	304.20	Cocaine Dependence
	304.80	Polysubstance Dependence
	_____	_____
	_____	_____
Axis II:	301.0	Paranoid Personality Disorder
	301.81	Narcissistic Personality Disorder
	301.7	Antisocial Personality Disorder
	301.9	Personality Disorder NOS
	_____	_____
	_____	_____

Appendix A

BIBLIOTHERAPY SUGGESTIONS

Anger Management

Ellis, A. (1977). *Anger: How to Live With and Without It.* Secaucus, NJ: Citadel Press.

Lerner, H. (1985). *The Dance of Anger: A Woman's Guide to Changing the Patterns of Intimate Relationships.* New York: Harper Perennial.

McKay, M.; Rogers, P.; and McKay, J. (1989). *When Anger Hurts.* Oakland, CA: New Harbinger.

Rosellini, G., and Worden, M. (1986). *Of Course You're Angry.* San Francisco: Harper Hazelden.

Rubin, T. I. (1969). *The Angry Book.* New York: Macmillan.

Smedes, L. (1991). *Forgive and Forget: Healing the Hurts We Don't Deserve.* San Francisco: Harper.

Tavris, C. (1989). *Anger: The Misunderstood Emotion.* New York: Touchstone Books.

Antisocial Behavior

Carnes, Patrick (1983). *Out of the Shadows: Understanding Sexual Addictions.* Minneapolis, MN: CompCare.

Katherine, A. (1991). *Boundaries: Where You End and I Begin.* New York: Simon & Schuster.

Williams, R., and Williams, V. (1993). *Anger Kills.* New York: Time Books.

Anxiety

Benson, H. (1975). *The Relaxation Response.* New York: William Morrow.

Davis, M.; Eshelman, E.; and McKay, M. (1988) *The Relaxation and Stress Reduction Workbook.* Oakland, CA: New Harbinger.

Hauck, Paul (1975). *Overcoming Worry and Fear.* Philadelphia, PA: Westminster Press.

Jeffers, S. (1987). *Feel the Fear and Do It Anyway.* San Diego, CA: Harcourt Brace Jovanovich.

Marks, Issac (1980). *Living with Fear: Understanding and Coping with Anxiety.* New York: McGraw-Hill.

Chemical Dependence

Alcoholics Anonymous (1975). *Living Sober.* New York: A. A. World Service.

Alcoholics Anonymous (1976). *Alcoholics Anonymous: The Big Book.* New York: A. A. World Service.

Carnes, P. (1989). *A Gentle Path Through the Twelve Steps.* Minneapolis, MN: CompCare.

Drews, T. R. (1980). *Getting Them Sober: A Guide for Those Living with Alcoholism.* South Plainfield, NJ: Bridge Publishing.

Johnson, V. (1980). *I'll Quit Tomorrow.* New York: Harper & Row.

Nuckals, C. (1989). *Cocaine: From Dependence to Recovery.* Blue Ridge Summit, PA: TAB Books.

Wilson, B. (1967). *As Bill Sees It.* New York: A. A. World Service.

Chemical Dependence—Relapse

Alcoholics Anonymous (1975). *Living Sober.* New York: A. A. World Service.

Alcoholics Anonymous (1976). *Alcoholics Anonymous: The Big Book.* New York: A. A. World Service.

Carnes, P. (1989). *A Gentle Path Through the Twelve Steps.* Minneapolis, MN: CompCare Publishing.

Drews, T. R. (1980). *Getting Them Sober: A Guide for Those Living with Alcoholism.* South Plainfield, NJ: Bridge Publishing.

Gorski, T., and Miller, M. (1986). *Staying Sober: A Guide to Relapse Prevention.* Independence, MO: Herald House Press.

Gorski, T. (1989–92). *The Staying Sober Workbook.* Independence, MO: Herald House Press.

Johnson, V. (1980). *I'll Quit Tomorrow.* New York: Harper & Row.

Larson, E. (1985). *Stage II Recovery: Life Beyond Addiction.* San Francisco, CA: Harper & Row.

Nuckals, C. (1989). *Cocaine: From Dependency to Recovery.* Blue Ridge Summit, PA: TAB Books.

Wilson, B. (1967). *As Bill Sees It.* New York: A. A. World Service.

Childhood Traumas

Black, C. (1980). *It Will Never Happen to Me.* Denver: MAC Publishing.

Bradshaw, J. (1990). *Homecoming.* New York: Bantam Books.

Gil, E. (1984). *Outgrowing the Pain: A Book for and About Adults Abused as Children*. New York: Dell Publishing.

Powell, J. (1969). *Why I'm Afraid to Tell You Who I Am*. Allen, TX: Argus Communications.

Whitfield, C. (1987). *Healing the Child Within*. Deerfield Beach, FL: Health Communications, Inc.

Cognitive Deficits

Ellis, A., and Harper, R. (1974). *A New Guide to Rational Living*. Hollywood, CA: Wilshire Books.

Dependency

Alberti, R., and Emmons, M. (1990). *Your Perfect Right*. San Luis Obispo, CA: Impact.

Beattie, M. (1987). *Codependent No More: How to Stop Controlling Others & Start Caring for Yourself*. San Francisco: Harper.

Drews. T. R. (1980). *Getting Them Sober: A Guide for Those Living with Alcoholism*. South Plainfield, NJ: Bridge Publishing.

Helmfelt, R.; Minirth, F.; and Meier, P. (1985). *Love Is a Choice*. Nashville, TN: Nelson.

Norwood, R. (1985). *Women Who Love Too Much*. Los Angeles: Tarcher.

Walker, L. (1979). *The Battered Woman*. New York: Harper & Row.

Whitfield, C. (1990). *A Gift to Myself: A Personal Guide to Healing My Child Within*. Deerfield Beach, FL: Health Communications, Inc.

Whitfield, C. (1993). *Boundaries and Relationships: Knowing, Protecting and Enjoying the Self*. Deerfield Beach, FL: Health Communications, Inc.

Depression

Burns, D. (1980). *Feeling Good: The New Mood Therapy*. New York: Signet.

Burns, D. (1989). *The Feeling Good Handbook*. New York: Plume.

Dyer, W. (1974). *Your Erroneous Zones*. New York: Funk & Wagnalls.

Frankl, V. (1959). *Man's Search for Meaning*. New York: Simon & Schuster.

Geisel, T. (1990). *Oh, The Places You'll Go*. New York: Random House.

Hallinan, P. K. (1976). *One Day at a Time*. Minneapolis, MN: CompCare.

Hazelden Staff (1991). *Each Day a New Beginning*. Center City, MN: Hazelden.

Knauth, P. (1977). *A Season in Hell*. New York: Pocket Books.

Dissociation

Grateful Members of Emotional Health Anonymous (1982). *The Twelve Steps for Everyone . . . Who Really Wants Them*. Minneapolis, MN: CompCare.

Eating Disorder

Hollis, J. (1985). *Fat Is a Family Affair.* New York: Harper & Row.

Educational Deficits

de Boro, E. (1982). *de Boro's Thinking Course.* New York: Facts of Life Publishing.

Sandstrom, R. (1990). *The Ultimate Memory Book.* Granada, CA: Stepping Stones Books.

Family Conflicts

Bloomfield, H., and Felder, L. (1983). *Making Peace with Your Parents.* New York: Random House.

Faber, A., and Mazlish, E. (1987). *Siblings Without Rivalry.* New York: Norton.

Ginott, H. (1969). *Between Parent and Child.* New York: Macmillan.

Steinberg, L., and Levine, A. (1990). *You and Your Adolescent: A Parents' Guide for Ages 10–20.* New York: Harper Perennial.

Female Sexual Dysfunction

Barbach, L. (1982). *For Each Other: Sharing Sexual Intimacy.* New York: Doubleday.

Comfort, A. (1991). *The New Joy of Sex.* New York: Crown.

Heiman, J., and LoPiccolo, J. (1988). *Becoming Orgasmic: A Sexual Growth Program for Women.* New York: Prentice-Hall.

Kaplan, H. S. (1975). *The Illustrated Manual of Sex Therapy.* New York: Quadrangle, The New York Times Book Co.

McCarthy, B., and McCarthy, E. (1984). *Sexual Awareness.* New York: Carroll & Graf.

Penner, C., and Penner C. (1981). *The Gift of Sex.* Waco, TX: Word.

Valins, L. (1992). *When a Woman's Body Says No to Sex: Understanding and Overcoming Vaginismus.* New York: Penguin.

Zibergeld, B. (1992). *The New Male Sexuality.* New York: Bantam.

Grief/Loss Unresolved

Colgrove, M. (1991). *How to Survive the Loss of a Love.* Los Angeles: Prelude Press.

Kushner, H. (1981). *When Bad Things Happen to Good People.* New York: Schocken Books.

Lewis, C. S. (1961). *A Grief Observed.* New York: The Seabury Press.

Rando, T. (1991). *How to Go on Living When Someone You Love Dies.* New York: Bantam.

Schiff, N. (1977). *The Bereaved Parent.* New York: Crown Publication.

Smedes, L. (1982). *How Can It Be All Right When Everything Is All Wrong.* San Francisco: Harper.

Westberg, G. (1962). *Good Grief.* Philadelphia: Augsburg Fortress Press.

Wolterstorff, N. (1987). *Lament for a Son.* Grand Rapids, MI: Eerdmans.

Impulse Control Disorder

Helmstetter, S. (1986). *What to Say When You Talk to Yourself.* New York: Fine Communications.

Kelly, K., and Ramundo, P. (1994). *You Mean I'm Not Lazy, Stupid or Crazy: A Self-Help Book for Adults with Attention Deficit Disorder.* Cincinnati, OH: Tyrell & Jerem Press.

Wander, P. (1987). *The Hyperactive Child, Adolescent and Adult.* New York: Oxford.

Intimate Relationship Conflicts

Bach, G., and Wyden, P. (1976). *The Intimate Enemy: How to Fight Fair in Love and Marriage.* New York: Avon Books.

Fisher, B. (1981). *ReBuilding: When Your Relationship Ends.* San Luis Obispo, CA: Impact.

Fromm, E. (1956). *The Art of Loving.* New York: Harper & Row.

Gorski, T. (1993). *Getting Love Right: Learning the Choices of Healthy Intimacy.* New York: Simon & Schuster.

Gray, J. (1993). *Men and Women and Relationships: Making Peace with the Opposite Sex.* Hillsboro, OR: Beyond Words.

Harley, W. (1994). *His Needs, Her Needs: Building an Affair-Proof Marriage.* Grand Rapids, MI: Revell.

Hendrix, H. (1988). *Getting the Love You Want.* New York: Henry Holt.

Lerner, H. (1989). *The Dance of Intimacy: A Woman's Guide to Courageous Acts of Change in Key Relationships.* New York: Harper Perennial.

Lindbergh, A. (1955). *A Gift from the Sea.* New York: Pantheon.

Legal Conflicts

Carnes, P. (1983). *Out of the Shadows: Understanding Sexual Addictions.* Minneapolis, MN: CompCare.

Williams, R., and Williams, V. (1993). *Anger Kills.* New York: Time Books.

Low Self-Esteem

Burns, D. (1993). *Ten Days to Self Esteem!* New York: William Morrow.

Helmstetter, S. (1986). *What to Say When You Talk to Yourself.* New York: Fine Communications.

McKay, M., and Fanning, P. (1987). *Self-Esteem.* Oakland, CA: New Harbinger.

Male Sexual Dysfunction

Comfort, A. (1991). *The New Joy of Sex*. New York: Crown.
Kaplan, H. S. (1975). *The Illustrated Manual of Sex Therapy*. New York: Quadrangle, The New York Times Book Co.
McCarthy, B., and McCarthy, E.(1984). *Sexual Awareness*. New York: Carroll & Graf.
Penner, C., and Penner, C. (1981). *The Gift of Sex*. Waco, TX: Word.
Zilbergeld, B. (1992). *The New Male Sexuality*. New York: Bantam.

Mania or Hypomania

Grateful Members of Emotional Health Anonymous (1987). *The Twelve Steps for Everyone . . . Who Really Wants Them*. Minneapolis, MN: CompCare.

Medical Issues

Friedman, M., and Ulmer, P. (1984). *Treating Type A Behavior and Your Heart*. New York: Alfred Knopf.

Obsessive-Compulsive Behaviors

Foa, E., and Wilson, R. (1991). *S.T.O.P. Obsessing: How to Overcome Your Obsessions and Compulsions*. New York: Bantam Books.
Levenkron, S. (1991). *Obsessive-Compulsive Disorders*. New York: Warner Books.

Paranoid Ideation

Cudney, M., and Hard, R. (1991). *Self-Defeating Behaviors*. San Fransisco: Harper Collins.
Ross, J. (1994). *Triumph over Fear*. New York: Bantam Books.

Phobia-Panic/Agoraphobia

Gold, M. (1988). *The Good News About Panic, Anxiety, and Phobias*. New York: Villard/Random House.
Marks, I. (1980). *Living with Fear: Understanding and Coping with Anxiety*. New York: McGraw-Hill.
Swede, S., and Jaffe, S. (1987). *The Panic Attack Recovery Book*. New York: New American Library.
Wilson, R. (1986). *Don't Panic: Taking Control of Anxiety Attacks*. New York: Harper & Row.

Psychoticism

Torrey, M. D., and Fuller, E. (1988). *Surviving Schizophrenia: A Family Manual.* New York: Harper & Row.

Sexual Abuse

Bass, E., and Davis, L. (1988). *The Courage to Heal: A Guide for Women Survivors of Child Sexual Abuse.* San Francisco: HarperCollins.

Bradshaw, J. (1988). *Healing the Shame That Binds You.* Deerfield Beach, FL: Health Communications, Inc.

Davis, L. (1990). *The Courage to Heal Workbook: For Men & Women Survivors of Child Sexual Abuse.* San Francisco: HarperCollins.

Forward, S., and Buck, C. (1978). *Betrayal of Innocence: Incest and Its Devastation.* New York: Penguin Books.

Fossum, M. A., and Mason, M. J. (1986). *Facing Shame: Families in Recovery.* New York: Norton.

Gil, E. (1984). *Outgrowing the Pain: A Book for and About Adults Abused as Children.* New York: Dell Publishing.

Kaufman, G. (1992). *Shame: The Power of Caring.* Rochester, VT: Schenkman Books.

Sleep Disturbance

Dotto, L. (1990). *Losing Sleep: How Your Sleeping Habits Affect Your Life.* New York: William Morrow.

Hewish, J. (1985). *Relaxation.* Chicago: NTC Publishing Group.

Social Discomfort

Bradshaw, J. (1988). *Healing the Shame That Binds You.* Deerfield Beach, FL: Health Communications, Inc.

Burns, D. (1985). *Intimate Connections: The New Clinically Tested Program for Overcoming Loneliness.* New York: William Morrow.

Fossum, M. A., and Mason, M. J. (1986). *Facing Shame: Families in Recovery.* New York: Norton.

Nouwen, H. (1975). *Reaching Out.* New York: Doubleday.

Zimbardo, P. (1987). *Shyness: What It Is and What to Do About It.* Reading, PA: Addison-Wesley.

Somatization

Benson, H. (1980). *The Mind-Body Effect.* New York: Simon & Schuster.

Grateful Members of Emotional Health Anonymous (1987). *The Twelve Steps for Everyone . . . Who Really Wants Them.* Minneapolis, MN: CompCare.

Spiritual Confusion

Helmfelt, R., and Fowler, R. (1990). *Serenity: A Companion for 12 Step Recovery*. Nashville, TN: Nelson.

Peck, M. S. (1978). *The Road Less Traveled*. New York: Simon & Schuster.

Peck, M. S. (1993). *Further Along the Road Less Traveled*. New York: Simon & Schuster.

Presnall, L. (1959). *Search for Serenity: And How to Achieve It*. Salt Lake City, UT: V.A.F. Publishing.

Suicidality

Butler, P. (1991). *Talking to Yourself: Learning the Language of Self-Affirmation*. New York: Stein and Day.

Hutschnecker, A. (1951). *The Will to Live*. New York: Cornerstone Library.

Seligman, M. (1990). *Learned Optimism: The Skill to Conquer Life's Obstacles, Large and Small*. New York: Pocket Books.

Type A Behavior

Friedman, M., and Olmer, D. (1984). *Treating Type A Behaviors and Your Heart*. New York: Alfred Knopf.

Glasser, W. (1976). *Positive Addiction*. San Francisco: HarperCollins.

Peck, M. S. (1978). *The Road Less Traveled*. New York: Simon & Schuster.

Peck, M. S. (1993). *Further Along the Road Less Traveled*. New York: Simon & Schuster.

Robinson, B. (1993). *Overdoing It*. Deerfield Beach, FL: Health Communications, Inc.

Vocational Stress

Bolles, R. (1992). *What Color Is Your Parachute?* Berkeley, CA: Ten-Speed Press.

Charland, R. (1993). *Career Shifting: Starting Over in a Changing Economy*. Holbrook, MA: Bob Adams.

Jandt, F. (1985). *Win-Win Negotiating: Turning Conflict into Agreement*. New York: John Wiley & Sons.

Weiss, R. (1990). *Staying the Course: The Emotional and Social Lives of Men Who Do Well at Work*. New York: Free Press.

Appendix B

INDEX OF DSM-IV CODES ASSOCIATED WITH PRESENTING PROBLEMS

Academic Problem   **V62.3**
    Educational Deficits

Adjustment Disorder with Anxiety   **309.24**
    Anxiety
    Intimate Relationship Conflicts
    Vocational Stress

Adjustment Disorder with Depressed Mood   **309.0**
    Depression
    Grief/Loss Unresolved
    Intimate Relationship Conflicts
    Vocational Stress

Adjustment Disorder with Disturbance of Conduct   **309.3**
    Antisocial Behavior
    Grief/Loss Unresolved
    Legal Conflicts

Adult Antisocial Behavior   **V71.01**
    Chemical Dependence
    Legal Conflicts

Agoraphobia without History of Panic Disorder   **300.22**
    Phobia-Panic/Agoraphobia

Alcohol Abuse   **305.00**
    Chemical Dependence
    Chemical Dependence—Relapse

Alcohol Dependence   **303.90**
    Antisocial Behavior
    Chemical Dependence
    Chemical Dependence—Relapse
    Cognitive Deficits
    Dissociation
    Family Conflicts
    Legal Conflicts
    Medical Issues
    Obsessive-Compulsive Behaviors
    Sexual Abuse
    Vocational Stress

Alcohol-Induced Persisting Amnestic Disorder   **291.1**
    Chemical Dependence
    Chemical Dependence—Relapse
    Cognitive Deficits

The diagnostic codes are used with permission from *Diagnostic and Statistical Manual of Mental Disorders, Fourth Edition,* 1994, Washington, DC: American Psychiatric Association.

Alcohol-Induced Persisting Dementia   291.2
  Chemical Dependence
  Chemical Dependence—Relapse
  Cognitive Deficits

Amnestic Disorder Due to (Axis III Disorder)   294.0
  Cognitive Deficits

Amnestic Disorder NOS   294.8
  Cognitive Deficits

Anorexia Nervosa   307.1
  Eating Disorder

Antisocial Personality Disorder   301.7
  Anger Management
  Antisocial Behavior
  Chemical Dependence
  Chemical Dependence—Relapse
  Childhood Traumas
  Family Conflicts
  Impulse Control Disorder
  Legal Conflicts
  Vocational Stress

Anxiety Disorder NOS   300.00
  Anxiety
  Family Conflicts
  Intimate Relationship Conflicts
  Obsessive-Compulsive Behaviors
  Spiritual Confusion

Avoidant Personality Disorder   301.82
  Dependency
  Obsessive-Compulsive Behaviors
  Sexual Abuse
  Social Discomfort

Bereavement   V62.82
  Depression
  Grief/Loss Unresolved

Bipolar Disorder NOS   296.80
  Mania or Hypomania

Bipolar I Disorder   296.xx
  Anger Management
  Depression
  Low Self-Esteem
  Mania or Hypomania
  Psychoticism
  Suicidal Ideation

Bipolar II Disorder   296.89
  Anger Management
  Depression
  Low Self-Esteem
  Mania or Hypomania
  Psychoticism
  Suicidal Ideation

Body Dysmorphic Disorder   300.7
  Somatization

Borderline Intellectual Functioning   V62.89
  Educational Deficits

Borderline Personality Disorder   301.83
  Anger Management
  Dependency
  Family Conflicts
  Impulse Control Disorder
  Suicidal Ideation

Brief Psychotic Disorder   298.8
  Psychoticism

Bulimia Nervosa   307.51
  Eating Disorder

Cannabis Abuse   305.20
  Chemical Dependence

Cannabis Dependence   304.30
  Chemical Dependence
  Chemical Dependence—Relapse
  Cognitive Deficits

Circadian Rhythm Sleep Disorder   307.45
  Sleep Disturbance

**Female Dyspareunia Due to
(Axis III Disorder)**   **625.0**
   Female Sexual Dysfunction

**Female Hypoactive Sexual
Desire Disorder Due to (Axis III
Disorder)**   **625.8**
   Female Sexual Dysfunction

**Female Orgasmic
Disorder**   **302.73**
   Female Sexual Dysfunction

**Female Sexual Arousal
Disorder**   **302.72**
   Female Sexual Dysfunction

**Generalized Anxiety
Disorder**   **300.02**
   Anxiety
   Childhood Trauma
   Sexual Abuse
   Type A Behavior

**Hypoactive Sexual Desire
Disorder**   **302.71**
   Female Sexual Dysfunction
   Male Sexual Dysfunction

Hypochondriasis   **300.7**
   Medical Issues
   Somatization

**Impulse Control Disorder
NOS**   **312.30**
   Impulse Control Disorder

**Intermittent Explosive
Disorder**   **312.34**
   Anger Management
   Antisocial Behavior
   Chemical Dependence
   Family Conflicts
   Impulse Control Disorder
   Intimate Relationship Conflicts

Kleptomania   **312.32**
   Impulse Control Disorder
   Legal Conflicts

**Major Depressive
Disorder**   **296.xx**
   Childhood Trauma
   Depression
   Low Self-Esteem
   Obsessive-Compulsive Behaviors
   Psychoticism
   Sexual Abuse
   Sleep Disturbance
   Social Discomfort
   Spiritual Confusion
   Vocational Stress

**Major Depressive Disorder,
Recurrent**   **296.3x**
   Depression
   Grief/Loss Unresolved
   Suicidal Ideation

**Major Depressive Disorder,
Single Episode**   **296.2x**
   Depression
   Grief/Loss Unresolved
   Suicidal Ideation

**Maladaptive Health Behaviors
Affecting (Axis III Disorder) 316**
   Medical Issues

**Male Dyspareunia Due to (Axis
III Disorder)**   **608.89**
   Male Sexual Dysfunction

Male Erectile Disorder   **302.72**
   Male Sexual Dysfunction

**Male Erectile Disorder Due to
(Axis III Disorder)**   **607.84**
   Male Sexual Dysfunction

**Male Hypoactive Sexual Desire
Disorder Due to (Axis III
Disorder)**   **608.89**
   Male Sexual Dysfunction

Male Orgasmic Disorder   **302.74**
   Male Sexual Dysfunction

Chemical Dependence—Relapse
Family Conflicts
Sexual Abuse
Vocational Stress

**Posttraumatic Stress
Disorder**   **309.81**
   Anger Management
   Chemical Dependence
   Chemical Dependence—Relapse
   Childhood Traumas
   Intimate Relationship Conflicts
   Sleep Disturbance
   Social Discomfort

Premature Ejaculation   **302.75**
   Male Sexual Dysfunction

Primary Hypersomnia   **307.44**
   Sleep Disturbance

Primary Insomnia   **307.42**
   Sleep Disturbance

**Psychological Symptoms
Affecting (Axis III Disorder)**   **316**
   Medical Issues

Pyromania   **312.33**
   Impulse Control Disorder

Reading Disorder   **315.00**
   Educational Deficits

Schizoaffective Disorder   **295.70**
   Depression
   Mania or Hypomania
   Psychoticism

**Schizoid Personality
Disorder**   **301.20**
   Intimate Relationship Conflicts
   Social Discomfort

Schizophrenia   **295.xx**
   Psychoticism

**Schizophrenia, Paranoid
Type**   **295.30**
   Paranoid Ideation
   Psychoticism

**Schizophreniform
Disorder**   **295.40**
   Psychoticism

**Schizotypal Personality
Disorder**   **301.22**
   Paranoid Ideation
   Social Discomfort

**Sedative, Hypnotic, or
Anxiolytic Dependence**   **304.10**
   Chemical Dependence
   Obsessive-Compulsive Behaviors

**Sexual Abuse of Child
(995.53, Victim)**   **V61.21**
   Childhood Traumas
   Female Sexual Dysfunction
   Male Sexual Dysfunction
   Sexual Abuse

**Sexual Aversion
Disorder**   **302.79**
   Female Sexual Dysfunction
   Male Sexual Dysfunction

Sexual Disorder NOS   **302.9**
   Female Sexual Dysfunction
   Male Sexual Dysfunction

Sleep Terror Disorder   **307.46**
   Sleep Disturbance

Sleepwalking Disorder   **307.46**
   Sleep Disturbance

Social Phobia   **300.23**
   Low Self-Esteem
   Paranoid Ideation
   Social Discomfort

Build your Treatment Planning Library with these time-saving resources from John Wiley & Sons:

* **The Child and Adolescent Psychotherapy Treatment Planner**
  240pp ◆ Paper ◆ 0471-15647-7 ◆ $39.95
* **The Continuum of Care Treatment Planner**
  208pp ◆ Paper ◆ 0471-19568-5 ◆ $39.95
* **The Couples Therapy Treatment Planner**
  208pp ◆ Paper ◆ 0471-24711-1 ◆ $39.95
* **The Chemical Dependence Treatment Planner**
  208pp ◆ Paper ◆ 0471-23795-7 ◆ $39.95
* **The Employee Assistance (EAP) Treatment Planner**
  176pp ◆ Paper ◆ 0471-24709-X ◆ $39.95
* **The Pastoral Counseling Therapy Treatment Planner**
  208pp ◆ Paper ◆ 0471-25416-9 ◆ $39.95
* **TheraScribe® 3.0 for Windows®:** *The Computerized Assistant to Psychotherapy Treatment Planning*
  Single User/0471-18415-2 ◆ $450.00
  Network/0471-18416-0 ◆ Call 1-800-0655 (x4708) for pricing
* **TheraBiller w/TheraScheduler™:** *The Computerized Mental Health Office Manager*
  Single User/0471-17102-2 ◆ $599.95
  Network, Call 1-800-0655 (x4708) for pricing

**Order the above products through your local bookseller, or by calling
1-800-225-5945 from 8:30 a.m. to 5:30 p.m., est.
Or visit our web site: www.wiley.com/therascribe**

For more information about on all of our **PRACTICE PLANNERS**™ resources, fill in this coupon, and mail it to: M. Fellin, John Wiley & Sons, Inc., 605 Third Avenue, New York, NY 10158.

Please send me information on:

- ❏ The Employee Assistance (EAP) Treatment Planner
- ❏ The Child & Adolescent Treatment Planner
- ❏ The Chemical Dependence Treatment Planner
- ❏ The Couples Therapy Treatment Planner
- ❏ The Pastoral Counseling Treatment Planner
- ❏ The Continuum of Care Treatment Planner
- ❏ The Group Therapy Treatment Planner
- ❏ The Older Adult Treatment Psychotherapy Treatment Planner
- ❏ TheraScribe® 3.0
- ❏ TheraBiller™ w/TheraScheduler™

Name _____

Affiliation _____

Address _____

_____

City/State/Zip _____

Phone _____

WILEY

TheraBiller with TheraScheduler™

The Computerized Mental Health Office Manager

TheraBiller w/TheraScheduler™ is our new Windows®-based software package designed specifically to help you manage your mental health practice....

Powerful...
- TheraBiller™ with TheraScheduler™ integrates seamlessly with TheraScribe® 3.0: The Computerized Assistant to Psychotherapy Treatment Planning. Although each program can be used independently, by using them in cooperatively you'll get a complete office management system, with automatic common data sharing and one-button toggling
- Completes pre-printed or program-generated HCFA forms, and produces easy-to-read, professional-looking invoices and aged accounts receivable reports
- Tracks managed care information (sessions authorized, sessions used, capitated fees, hourly fees, etc.)
- Built-in electronic billing compatibility (claims module interfaces with InStream Provider Network™ or MedE America™ for on-line commerce)
- Electronic cardex which prints mailing labels and tracks contact information

Flexible...
- Robust reporting options — print or preview billing summaries and usage statistics by provider, patient, or time-frame
- Full quick-reference DSM-IV and CPT code libraries (including new G-codes)
- Data export to Quicken® and MicroSoft Money®, as well as common spreadsheet and accounting programs (e.g., Excel®, Peachtree®, etc.)
- Perfect for solo providers or large group practices (the stand-alone version handles an unlimited number of providers, and a network version is also available)

User-Friendly...
- Features the same intuitive interface as Wiley's best-selling TheraScribe ®3.0.
- Includes a handy Billing Wizard to guide you through the billing process and a Report Wizard that helps you select report parameters
- Built-in appointment book, with daily, weekly, monthly scheduling for an unlimited number of providers— updates automatically when you book a session in TheraScribe® 3.0
- Password-protected to safeguard confidential data. Varying levels of data access may be assigned to each user

---

System Requirements
IBM®-compatible 486DX * 8 MB RAM (12MB recommended) * 10MB Hard Disk Space
VGA display (SVGA recommended) * Windows® 3.1

For more information on TheraBiller™, fill in this coupon, and mail it to: M. Fellin, John Wiley & Sons, Inc., 605 Third Avenue, New York, NY 10158.

Name _____

Affiliation _____

Address _____

City/State/Zip _____

Phone _____

Visit our web site and download a free demo: www.wiley.com/therabiller

⟨W⟩ WILE
Publishers Since 18